Why Polls Don't Matter in the Age of Trump

John Pope

Published by John Pope

www.JohnHPope.com

Name: John Pope, Author

Title: Why Polls Don't Matter in the Age of Trump

First Edition

ISBN (paperback) 978-0-9983008-2-5

ISBN (ebook) 978-0-9983008-3-2

Table of Contents

Acknowledgements

This book is dedicated to

my very best friend,

Kevin Cotnoir.

He was taken from us way too soon.

From the weather, to music, to politics, I will surely miss our conversations. He was a dear friend indeed.

Rest peacefully old friend.

Trump Derangement Syndrome

On December 5, 2003, the late, great Charles Krauthammer, in an article for Townhall, discusses his discovery of a new psychiatric syndrome that he labeled Bush Derangement Syndrome. His definition:

> *Bush Derangement Syndrome: the acute onset of paranoia in otherwise normal people in reaction to the policies, the presidency -- nay -- the very existence of George W. Bush.*

This was a condition experienced by many liberals on the left who did not agree with the policies of President Bush. This disagreement became completely illogical, with many on the left creating false narratives of things that *could* or *might* happen *if* President Bush wanted to lead the country astray. Then the reporting would morph to these possibilities being reported as fact. The result was paranoia and the belief that the world as we know it is coming to an end.

Obviously, that didn't happen. The financial crisis and the Great Recession did happen at the end of President Bush's presidency, and President Obama used that as his reasoning of why the economy never took off during his administration.

One of the main contributors to the Great Recession was the housing market crash. The crash occurred mainly because liberals had removed the safeguards that prevented people from getting housing loans that they really could not afford. It is a nice dream that everyone should own a house, but the fact is, many people did not have the available funds to pay a mortgage *and* maintain a house. But that is a different book ☺

Charles Krauthammer also diagnosed the same condition for President Trump, labelling it Trump Derangement Syndrome. It is paranoia and hatred for all things Trump. It is Bush Derangement Syndrome times 10.

If President Trump, or someone in his administration eats at a restaurant, then people with Trump Derangement Syndrome believe that the restaurant owner, for having the audacity to not deny the President or his associates a meal, should be punished by boycotting that restaurant.

If a family member of President Trump owns a business, then people with Trump Derangement Syndrome are full believers in guilt by association, and that family member should have their businesses boycotted.

If President Trump offers a policy opinion, then politicians with Trump Derangement Syndrome will immediately issue statements that they completely and utterly disagree, even though they previously and publicly agreed to that very same position.

If a family member has Trump Derangement Syndrome, they will not allow any Trump supporters in their home, even if the Trump supporter is their mother. I have personally witnessed this.

When Trump Derangement Syndrome is analyzed, it is all based on fear, hatred, and completely illogical thinking.

Is the fear, hatred, and illogical thinking justified?

Let's begin by discussing Donald Trump. I want to be brutally honest. He is a gruff, rough speaking, in-your-face, blatant, and to-the-point kind of man. He doesn't mince words, and his vocabulary is extremely limited.

He was born into money. His father gave him loans to begin his own business. It seems that the reported amounts vary, but the loans were somewhere in the range of one million to fifteen million dollars. This is an astronomical amount to most of us, but the real question is, what did Trump do with the money? Of course, the answer is, he built a multi-billion dollar company.

People who want to minimize the success of Trump will point to the Forbes 400 List of 2005, which indicate that Trump was worth about 2.7 billion dollars. This directly contradicts Trump's own statements in which he indicates that his worth is closer to 5 billion dollars.

However, the Forbes 400 List for 2015, indicates that Trump's worth is around 4.5 billion dollars, which aligns to Trump's claims.

This is one of the symptoms of Trump Derangement Syndrome. The tendency of a person to pick and choose from the available facts with a goal of disparaging Trump.

Many people believe that if they were given the money that Trump had to begin his business, then they would be just as successful. But history is littered with lottery winners, estate bequeathments, and wannabe entrepreneurs that completely disprove this. In business, you do need money to get the business off the ground, and there are many successful entrepreneurs, but very few can claim the success that businessmen like Donald Trump achieve.

Was Trump fortunate that he had a wealthy father that could loan him the money? Yes, and so what? Almost all of us have had parents that have given us help.

I was not fortunate in this respect since my family was just a working class, paycheck-to-paycheck family. But I had quite a few friends over the years whose parents gave them down payments on homes, usually tens of thousands of dollars. Were they fortunate? You bet they were. Was I envious? Absolutely, but I never held them in low regard. I never thought poorly of them because of their fortunate circumstances.

The fact is, their parents worked hard and became successful. Their parents could then use their wealth to give their children a head start in life. This is part of the American dream. To be able to build yourself up, increase your wealth, and then help your children to have a better life.

My parents struggled. They couldn't afford to give me a down payment on a home, but they helped me to become more comfortable than they were. In turn, I hope to help my own children to be more comfortable than I was. In Trump's case, it is only a matter of degrees. Most of us help or get help in the form of thousands, or tens of thousands of dollars. Trump's father was able to help in the form of millions. This is the American dream in action. We can be envious, but we should never be jealous.

What about Trumps vocabulary? Have you ever heard anyone use the adjective "beautiful" in so many ways? The "beautiful wall", "big, beautiful hands", a "beautiful bill", "young and beautiful lives". The list is endless.

Let's approach this from a couple of different perspectives. The first is the idea of being "Presidential". The suave, sophisticated politician who speaks eloquently. The politician who always takes the high road. The politician who doesn't respond to silly insults from media or members of the entertainment community. The politician who meets with other world leaders and never rocks the boat. The politician who always compliments other leaders and never berates them publicly. This is the politician who is above the fray. This is the politician that we have come to expect from the President of the United States. This is the politician who looks fabulous on camera. This is the politician who never makes us cringe. This is the politician who never gets anything done.

Outwardly, these are all fine qualities. They exude the characteristics that have become the basis for the stuffy, clichéd, political atmosphere in the United States and abroad.

When our presidents engage in world politics, we don't expect results, we just expect them to be presidential. In an attempt to not embarrass us, and in an attempt to not "harm" our relationships with other countries, our presidents are expected to follow the policies and procedures that have been ingrained into our psyche.

An analogy would be watching the Royal Wedding in England. There are policies, procedures, and routines that *must* be adhered to. To break from tradition would be disrespectful, and thus harmful, to the community at large. This is the same type of "Presidential" political mores that we have come to expect. In some cases, that we have come to demand.

And what is the glue that links our "Presidential Standard" together? What is the one thing that shows up in all of our definitions? It is the word "politician".

Our vision of a "Presidential" president is the consummate politician. The suave, sophisticated, eloquent speaker, who can precisely and concisely explain their position. Can be politically correct and never hurt anyone's feelings. Can agree with and pander to one group, while agreeing with and pandering to another group that holds the exact opposite position. Can meet with world leaders and never tell them the truth, lest they might no longer want to be our friend. Ultimately, someone who is everything to everyone, but holds no real values themselves.

These "Presidential" Presidents are above the common people. Above the working class. Their presidential heads held high. All the while looking down on what they consider to be the ignorant masses. They know better than me, they know better than you, and regardless of what you think, they will do whatever they want while constantly blaming the other side when things are not going well. They relish the power that they wield, and in the end, they will do whatever it takes to hold on to that power.

All of our recent previous American presidents after Ronald Reagan fit into the "Presidential" standard in one way or another. Always following the rules. Always "looking" presidential.

Then there is the second perspective. Donald Trump. A non-eloquent, non-sophisticated speaker who bastardizes the English language on a regular basis. He uses imprecise language and is limited to a handful of adjectives. Sure, George W. Bush regularly bastardized the English language as well, but everything else fit into the "Presidential" standard.

President Trump was given the "Presidential Standard" from President Obama. Trump took it, read it, ripped it up and threw it in the oval office trash can.

Trump tells the American people, as well as foreign leaders, the truth on behalf of America. In plain, simplistic language. His vocabulary may be limited, but when he speaks, everyone knows what he means.

Interestingly, because he truly has the best interest of America and her citizens in mind, he becomes eloquent in his non-eloquence and becomes sophisticated in his non-sophistication. Once one realizes the tactics behind the bluster, and the positive results, it becomes easy to forgive the simplistic outward appearance.

Trump is the type of president who stands up to the leaders of rogue regimes who use bully tactics to instill fear into America and her allies. In the past, these foreign leaders have shouted and thrashed like a schoolyard bully, and the world capitulated. Always worried that we might anger them and start a war.

Trump's style is diametrically different. He stands up to these bullies and confronts them head on. Ultimately coming out on top because he is a bigger bully than them, and because he knows how to negotiate by utilizing the substantial influence of the United States.

The world hates bullies. Bullies that take advantage of the weak and defenseless. The kid stealing your child's lunch money, or the dictator that threatens nuclear war.

In the case of world politics, the weak and defenseless are not only the citizens of these rogue regimes, but also the world leaders who capitulate and cater to the dictators. Their fear creates an ineptitude that borders on impotence.

These world leaders are so fearful of retribution by being strong, that their weakness allows the dictator to become more powerful. Through *lack* of action by the world community, these dictators maintain control, and become even more powerful.

But Trump is different. He can be a bully, there is no doubt. Except he redefines the term "bully", or rather, he adds a new definition.

Trump bullyism can be defined as:

"A bully who bullies the bully"

This seems odd at first, but if you think about it, it makes perfect sense. Trump does not bully people first, which is the classic definition of a bully. He is a counter puncher. If someone has something disparaging to say about Trump, or if something is said that he believes is untrue, then Trump fights back.

The "presidential president" would rise above the fray and say nothing. Constantly getting pounded by the other side. Never setting the record straight. Hoping that the media will dig deep and ultimately report the truth.

President Obama could easily act this way because the media was on his side. The media had nothing but good things to say about President Obama. If he did something good, they would endlessly loop it on their news shows. If he did something mediocre, they would spin it as a momentous accomplishment. If he did something bad, they just wouldn't cover it at all.

The politicians, talking heads, Trump detractors, and even some of his supporters believe that he should not respond to every little remark. That responding in kind, or defending yourself at all is beneath the Presidency. They believe that Trump should hold his head high, above all of the disparaging comments, the misstatements of fact, and the unfounded accusations. They say that this is what President's do, but President Trump believes otherwise.

I must admit that sometimes when I read some of President Trump's tweets, I visibly cringe. However, for the most part, I get it. No president has ever had to put up with the constant onslaught of so many people trying to discredit him.

I use the term "so many people" as a relative term. In the scope of things, the amount of people saying bad things to and about Donald Trump is vastly larger than anything ever before. However, the number of these Trump haters are small when compared to the actual supporters of Donald Trump.

What Trump must deal with every day, is "the squeaky wheel" effect. When pulling your cart, one of the wheels begins to squeak. All of your wheels could use some oil, but the one you wind up oiling is the one that is squeaking. The one that gets your attention is the loudest wheel.

When it comes to President Trump, there are people who like him, people who don't care much for him, and people who absolutely hate him. There are relatively few haters when compared to the actual population of voters, but those few are the squeaky wheels. They are EXTREMELY loud and vociferous. And let's not forget that they have the power of the media and entertainers behind them.

The media and the entertainment industry cloud the reporting because they offer their twisted, nonfactual, uneducated views of President Trump. They are initiators and perpetrators of Trump Derangement Syndrome.

These people believe that it is Trump who is uneducated, immoral, uncaring, and is steering the country in the wrong direction. They believe that their view of the world is the *ONLY* view of the world.

President Trump was elected by the people, but to the media and the elites in the entertainment industry, the voice of the masses carries no weight and should be ignored. Only elite voices and the voices of those who agree with them count. If you disagree, then you are the enemy. You must be silenced so that the views that do not conform to their views cannot be propagated.

The group of people who have Trump Derangement Syndrome that amuse me the most are entertainers. Actors and singers who use their fame to spew their views on all of us. These people, and let's remember that they are only people just like you and me, have become incredibly rich and famous because of their talent.

But what is that talent? They have a natural God given gift of a beautiful voice, or they pretend to be other people in movies. I'll admit that they pretend to be other people really well, but they are not the people they pretend to be. It is fake.

Just because they can pretend to be a doctor in a TV show doesn't make them as knowledgeable as a doctor, and you probably wouldn't want them diagnosing your child if he or she was sick.

Just because they pretend to be a master computer programmer doesn't make them programming experts, and if we are ever invaded by aliens, we probably wouldn't call on them to crack the alien codes.

They are actors and actresses. They probably could not do the job that you do, but yet they make more money for one movie than most of us will ever see in our entire lives. In some cases, they make more money in one episode of a TV show than most of us will ever see in our entire lives.

However, because of their fame, we associate them with the characters that they play. When they pretend to be an educated professor, then somehow in our mind we equate them as being as smart as their character.

But they are not even saying their own thoughts. They are reading words from a page that someone else wrote. Then to add substance and truthfulness to their characters, they will observe real professors, real doctors, or whoever it is they will pretend to be.

These actors, actresses, and singers are not even close to who we envision them to be. In fact, we really know nothing about them. When you have an opinion about friends, family, or coworkers, it is because you interacted with them. You conversed with them. You get an idea of how intelligent they are. You get an idea of how caring they are. You get an idea of their political views. You can form this opinion because you know them through real interaction.

With entertainers, our opinion is based on a lie. It is based on who they portray and little sound bites of them being interviewed while promoting their new movie or cd. We feel like we know them because they are right in our living room, but when we hear stories about their real lives, we are always surprised. Think about the times you are watching television and you find yourself saying "He has a kid?", or "I didn't even know she was sick", or "Really? He lives in France?"

The list is endless because we really know nothing about these people. They are make believe people with whom we have created make believe lives.

So, when Robert De Niro, Whoopi Goldberg, or Madonna start telling me their views on how the country should be run, I immediately stop listening. These entertainers spew their hate and vitriol for President Trump, make inflammatory statements in an attempt to create violent dissent, succeed by persuading ignorant young adults to take to the streets and engage in riotous acts, and then go home to their multimillion-dollar estates, surrounded by an entourage of people who cater to their every whim and make them believe that they are second only to God.

These entertainers do have power. Especially over the young.

Winston Churchill once said,

"If you're not a liberal at age twenty, you have no heart. If you are still a liberal at age forty, you have no head"

The fact that most children and young adults are liberal makes sense. They have no life experience. Their mothers and fathers provide for them. They do not know what it means to provide for themselves, let alone for others in a family. So, it is easy to think that everyone should be provided for.

As they get older and start their own families, it becomes clear that to get ahead and provide the most for their family, they must do it on their own. As they become more successful, it becomes more apparent that people should use the government to lift them so that they can stand on their own, but not to carry them.

I was a liberal myself, until about half way through George W. Bush's presidency.

I worked hard to get where I was at that point in time, and I could see many people who used the government as a crutch. The government in return gave them just enough so that they did not need to stand on their own. In fact, the government put up barriers to prevent people from leaving the welfare rolls.

I personally experienced this around 1986. I was laid off and my wife at the time was working. We applied for food stamps to help out until I could get back to work. We were denied because my wife made too much. The welfare worker said that if we made fifty dollars less per month, then we would qualify for seven hundred dollars in benefits per month. I asked why we couldn't just subtract the fifty from the seven hundred. The welfare worker said it didn't work that way, and then instructed my wife at the time to miss four hours of work for two weeks and then submit those paystubs and try again, and we would be approved. We left and never went back.

On another occasion, a female friend of mine was collecting welfare benefits including cash, housing, and child care. She wanted to get a job and get off of welfare.

She found a job and asked the welfare department if she could just keep the child care benefits because she would not be able to afford the child care costs. Her welfare worker told her that if she starts her new job, she would no longer be eligible for any benefits including child care.

My friend would not be able to afford the child care, so it made financial sense for the benefit of her family to just stay on welfare. So she did.

Teachers are another tool that is being used in the liberal toolshed. Teachers used to have one goal. Educate our children.

Education meant learning English, mathematics, geography, science, and history. Nowadays, learning means adhering to a false curriculum created by elite people who have no real experience teaching.

Just like in the private sector, where people whose only experience are college doctorate degrees, these educators dictate policies which the real teachers know are wrong from actual experience. The big difference is that in the private sector, when things eventually go bad, the offenders are quickly replaced. If the company is quick enough in discovering the ineptitude of the decision makers, then the company might survive.

In the realm of education, these decision makers are there for life, and unfortunately, the focus has become indoctrination into the liberal logic, or should I say, the liberal illogic system rather than education.

A Pew Research Center study showed that in 2015, in the educational ranking of 15-year old's in 71 countries, the United States ranked twenty-fourth in science, twenty-fourth in reading, and a dismal thirty-eighth in mathematics.

Thirty-eighth in mathematics? Twenty-fourth in science? How can that be? How can our educational system be so flawed that the United States can't even rank anywhere near the top ten?

The answer is that liberalism and socialism have crept into our public-school systems. The focus is no longer at excelling in the fundamentals. The focus is on teaching children that their gender is not based on biology, but is a choice, and if Jimmy, who is a male student in the third grade, wants to be Jane from now on, then we should all be tolerant and understand his...her...its feelings.

Of course, we can't blame the third grader. It's his ignorant, liberal parents, and the foolish school system that actually goes along with it and fosters this kind of twisted thinking.

There has long been a debate on whether things like homosexuality or transsexuality are developed through nurture or nature. Nurture meaning outside influences and nature meaning you are born with it.

I personally believe that true homosexuals and transsexuals are born with these deep-seated feelings. It is entirely out of their control and we should always tolerate and never discriminate.

However, the school system has gone far beyond tolerance and they now embrace these ideas and actions.

Instead of stopping at toleration, these teachers, as early as third and fourth grade, are teaching about these controversial issues. Even worse, they are encouraging these ideas. Fostering these thoughts in young, impressionable minds. They are now influencing these young children. Rather than nature being the factor, the teachers are nurturing the students to experiment in these directions.

But why? School has always been about learning fundamental subject matter like mathematics, history, and science. The moral education and moral outlook of the students always came from the home. It is the parents who should be instilling *their* values into their children, not the state.

Since the schools focus on indoctrination and no longer focus on education, most public-school students today know nothing about their own history.

It makes for a cute and funny video clip when a reporter travels American college campuses and asks fundamental history questions like "Who fought in the Revolutionary War", or "Who won the American Civil War?" Most of the students asked give wrong answers. Not only wrong, but not even close. Answers that are in the wrong century or involving the wrong countries. The answers are funny in their absurdity. But on a much deeper level, it is an indicator of how our public schools teach, or rather, don't teach our young children. It is an indicator of the utter failure of the public-school system.

A more frightening reality, is that these college students who don't know anything at all about their own history, are now old enough to vote. That alone is a frightening proposition. Because now we have uninformed voters, who don't have a clue about history or how the world actually works, making decisions at the polls through their votes.

But wait! Wasn't that the liberal plan after all? That's what indoctrination is. Take over the educational system and instead of teaching the children educational subject matter, teach them how to be good liberals so that they will forever vote the liberals into power.

These college students are now at the forefront of Trump Derangement Syndrome. They are taking to the streets. If asked what they are demonstrating, they will say President Trump's policies. If pushed further and asked which policies in particular, they will say they don't want a racist and a misogynist president in the White House. When pushed yet further, and asked which policies in particular they believe to be misogynistic or discriminatory, the only answer they have is his handling of illegal immigration. When reminded that these are not President Trump's policies, but rather the law of the land enacted by congress, the young student's eyes usually gloss over, the mouth gapes open, and that's the end of the conversation.

These are the same students who bring this irrational thinking to the militant left, like Antifa, which stands for Anti Fascism. This group mobilizes quickly through social media and is militant in nature. They show up wearing masks, brandishing weapons, and have the obvious intention of creating a riot. They typically show up when a conservative speaks, especially on college campuses. The main goal when "protesting" a conservative speaker, is to prevent the conservative voice from ever being heard. To shut down the free speech system. To quiet every idea that Antifa does not agree with.

The Antifa movement is a direct result of the indoctrination of our students by our top-notch public-school system. They have taught our children that everyone is exactly equal, and that everyone should have exactly the same opportunities; that all opportunities should come at no cost, education should be free, and that healthcare should be free. When asked who should pay for all of these benefits, the enlightened student's response is always, "the government".

I have news for these ignorant young adults (as well as for Bernie Sanders). Nothing is free. If you are not paying for your education, then someone else is. If you are not paying for your health care, then someone else is.

These students often point to European countries as their social model, ignorant of the fact that the United States and their military might is the reason that these countries with lavish public benefits can exist in the first place.

We could be like the European countries and forego our military budget in favor of a socialist budget. We would all live happily ever after with everything being given to us for free. No more worries for health care, No more worries for educational expenses. No more worries at all. The only thing we need to do is stop funding the military and start funding social programs.

Fast forward fifty years. We are living in bliss. Everything is free. Our entitled students are happily living in the new United Utopia of America. All of our troops in other countries returned home long ago. Our military decimated to only a few thousand troops at the border.

But everything is free! That's what matters.

Uh oh. China and Russia didn't halt their military ambitions. They are now threatening the borders of the United Utopia of America, but there are no more soldiers. The planes and ships, decommissioned long ago to pay for the entitlements of the masses, are no longer available for defense. Not that it would matter, since China and Russia have fifty years of military development that we decided was unnecessary. We could ask Europe for help, but they are currently being annexed by China and Russia.

You may laugh at the ridiculousness of these thoughts, but this is just how quickly we could lose control of our country by ignoring the necessity of a strong military.

The liberals believe that we need only shower Russia and China with peace and love. They will then see the error of their ways and conform to the beauty of peace and love, and we can all wear togas, spend the day philosophizing, and spend the nights around the campfire, singing Kumbaya.

Any logical, informed person knows that this is a bunch of nonsensical BS. China and Russia would militarily take over the world in a heartbeat if they believed they could get away with it. Neither country is a democracy nor a republic, and they would exert their authoritarian rule on all of us if they had half the chance. The only thing preventing this is the military might of the United States of America.

College students just don't get it. The logic of the real world eludes them. These students believe they are fighting fascism, but it is they who are the fascists.

Two of the main tenets that define fascism are forcibly suppressing opposition and forcibly suppressing criticism. This is precisely what Antifa does. So, the hypocrisy is that the anti-fascists are actually the fascists, and conservatives are to be silenced at all costs.

Let me be clear that when I say conservative, I am not talking about White Supremacists. That is a political ploy of the left. To group all conservatives on the right as White Supremacists. This is far from the truth.

According to The Guardian, the White Supremacist movement held a protest at the White House on August 12, 2018. There were only twenty or thirty White Supremacist protestors, contrasted to thousands of anti-protesters. This is as it should be. There are very few White Supremacists because very few people believe in their doctrine.

Antifa, however, calls all conservatives, including President Trump, White Supremacists. By labelling them this way, Antifa creates the justification they need to use violence and rioting as a means to their end, which is total suppression of any idea or viewpoint that goes against their own. In other words, fascism.

When Antifa protests, or counter-protests, there are always buildings destroyed, cars set on fire, and people hurt on the other side. When conservatives protest, there are a lot of signs, walking, and a generally boring display of their viewpoints.

This attitude on the left to be able to do whatever they have to in order to suppress the other side has a direct correlation to Trump Derangement Syndrome. These liberals do not want to hear the arguments of the other side lest they will begin to make too much sense.

They do not want to hear logic. The fact that the economy is doing better than ever before, the fact that unemployment is the lowest among all groups then it has ever been is not a consideration.

Trump Derangement Syndrome is based on illogical thinking. People that hate President Trump can see nothing except hate. Everything that they claim that is wrong with Donald Trump, is precisely what is wrong with them. They are so consumed by their hate, that they cannot see any good, even when it is slapping them in the face.

I personally know several people that have stated that if you voted for Donald Trump, then you are no longer welcome in their house. Is that what the left has come to? If you have a different political view, they are willing to throw you out of their lives, just so they don't have to hear your point of view?

This behavior has no basis in logic. The logic of the left is non-existent. When a political debate occurs between a liberal and a conservative, the liberal comes armed with feelings. The conservative comes armed with facts.

As the debate progresses, the facts begin to make sense and the feelings become conflicted. To prevent this, the liberals do the only thing available in their arsenal. They stop the argument. They put their hands over their ears and scream "La la la la, I'm not listening to you." Finally, they throw you out of their house, telling you that you are no longer welcome so that they never have to listen to your pesky facts again.

Trump Derangement Syndrome is real. If you don't believe me, have a debate with your favorite liberal friend. Bring a few facts to the debate. You will quickly find yourself standing on the curb outside of their house, wondering what happened.

However, don't put too much thought into it. It is not logical and is not based on common sense. Just go home and hope that your friend will someday come to his or her senses.

Borders or No Borders?

Why do countries have borders anyway? Couldn't we just remove all borders and live in one, great big beautiful world where we all get along and everyone loves each other?

Anyone who even begins to believe that this is a remote a possibility is either misinformed, uneducated, or just plain ignorant.

History has shown us over and over again what can happen when one country becomes aggressive to their neighbors. If the kind neighboring countries are not well prepared, and do not have secure borders, then they will be overrun by the aggressive neighbor.

Impossible, you say? In this day and age, a thing like that just doesn't happen, right? Well, let's ask Ukraine.

During the Obama administration Ukraine was invaded by Russia. The eastern half of the country has now been annexed to Russia and it does not look like Russia has any intentions of returning the stolen land. So strong and secure borders are an absolute necessity if you want to maintain the freedom, rights, and privileges of any nation.

Look at the differences in countries around the world. The first, most obvious difference is language. Every country has their own language, and even the countries that have a common language still have their differences.

But language is the least of our worries. The main issues are ideology, culture, religion, definitions of freedom, social classes, work ethic, and these are only the beginning. In a word, we could say that the differences are everything. Every nation has their own set of values. Sure, we share many values, but there are always differences that would prevent us from simply combining two countries into one. Now imagine combining three countries, four countries, or a hundred countries.

It becomes absurd when you realize that Saudi Arabia has just allowed their women to drive automobiles in 2018. Can you imagine placing those types of limited values on women in the United States? No one would stand for it, and rightly so.

However, Saudi Arabia can do as they like in their own country. We don't agree with it. We can try to change their thinking. But in the end, they are not United States citizens. They do not have the same values that we do.

Now imagine that the liberals get their wish and tomorrow there are no longer any borders to the south of the United States. There are no border patrol agents, no ICE agents, and no police. The border checkpoints are torn down and there is only a wide-open highway.

It's a wonderful thought, do you agree? People peacefully walking and driving back and forth between the United States and Mexico. No terrorists, because everyone is now on the honor system.

As you enter into the United States it is agreed that you will harbor no ill will to the United States and its citizens, Scout's Honor. Maybe we'll make you sign a piece of paper that states that you promise to be good.

Everyone who enters the United States gets a job and contributes to the economy by doing all of those jobs that lazy Americans don't want to do. It's a utopia, just waiting to happen, if only we remove those pesky border barriers and useless law enforcement officials.

This is the future that liberals would have you believe is waiting to happen. All they need is to get control of government, and they can make this utopia a reality.

Do you see it now? Or are you like me?

Try as I might, I cannot reconcile removing borders with creating paradise. Sadly, if the borders were removed, all that I can see is a scene from The Walking Dead. Where swarms and swarms of people would come flooding through the open borders. Everyone fighting, and trying to grasp their piece of the American dream.

Except the American dream would quickly become a nightmare. There is only so much wealth that can be redistributed. The multitude of people that would come would not be college educated intellectuals trying to get a job as a professor at Harvard University. To the contrary, they would be the poorest, most impoverished, and least educated from South America and around the world.

These people would come across the border to take all of the jobs that Americans do not want to do. The problem is, the number of jobs that fit into this category of "jobs that Americans don't want to do" would vastly increase.

What the liberals never mention is the *reason* why Americans do not want these jobs. The answer of which, is simply... wages. These jobs include lawn care, building maintenance, residential and commercial painters, janitors, office cleaning, and many more. Americans no longer want these jobs because they can no longer make a decent wage. The illegal immigrants will work for much less than an American. Why wouldn't they? They don't have to pay income taxes.

But wait! The liberal left will say, they pay taxes because they need to steal a social security number in order to work. This stolen social security number will then be charged taxes through the United States government. Therefore, they pay taxes.

Hopefully, this stolen identity will not be your social security number or the social security number of someone dear to you. We have all had to deal with the United States government at some point. Imagine trying to disentangle an illegal immigrants' false claims from your own social security number? All I can envision is a lot of sleepless nights, a lot of attorney's fees, a lot of government fees, and a lot of threats from the government. Forget about the fact that what the illegal immigrant did was.. umm... ILLEGAL!

If you or I stole someone's identity and falsely used their social security number, we would probably be fined along with some jail time. But for the illegal immigrant, we didn't bother charging them with a crime when they illegally entered the country, so why start now? Besides, now they are contributing to our economy, right?

Not so fast. Another trick used by illegal immigrants is to falsely claim a high number of dependents on the W4 form. The government requires social security numbers for those children, but at this point the illegal immigrants have committed two crimes, so why not three?

Increasing the number of dependents decreases the amount of withholding, which in turn increases the amount that the illegal gets as take-home pay. It also decreases the amount that the illegal pays for taxes.

Some of you might be saying that this is preposterous. There are laws that prevent this from happening. My response would be, "of course there are laws". However, when shrugging off the notion that this type of social security number fraud cannot happen because there are checks and balances, as well as laws in place to prevent it, just remember that those same types of checks and balances and laws exist for someone who enters the country illegally. If the government is willing to turn a blind eye to immigrants entering illegally, is it really much of a stretch to then believe that these same liberal government officials wouldn't then turn a blind eye to social security number fraud?

This is not the only argument for why illegal immigrants pay their "fair share" of taxes. Another common liberal argument is that the illegal immigrants are adding to the economy by buying goods and services, and then paying the sales taxes on these goods. Really? Let's do the math.

A hard working American and an illegal immigrant pay the same amount of taxes for goods and services. That is true.

But a hard-working American pays ALL of his income taxes to the Federal Government and the State Government while the illegal immigrant pays a small portion based on deception. That doesn't sound equal to me.

Let us not forget the illegal immigrants who don't bother stealing the social security numbers. They just work "under the table" and receive pay without paying any taxes.

It is true that Americans will also do this, but at far higher wages. Alas, even the illegal method of working is no longer palatable to Americans because of the depressed wages.

The liberals always grasp onto something that they can spin as good or as a benefit. But allowing this behavior only further depresses the wages and drives them down to the point that only illegals are willing to work for that amount of pay.

Wages are not the only thing that suffers. Have you been to an emergency room recently?

When I was a kid, I made a few trips to the emergency room. A hair-line fracture in my forearm, asthma attacks, and several broken bone scares. Not a significant amount, but a few.

The difference between then and now, was that I went there when it was truly an emergency. Today is quite different. For illegals and citizens who can't or don't want to afford their own healthcare, the emergency room has become the doctor's office.

I always have only gone to the emergency room for emergencies, and I have always had to pay. Even back when I had a Health Maintenance Organization (HMO), I had co-pays. These HMO's were the best health insurance plans that I have ever had. They had reasonable co-pays. Twenty dollars for a doctor visit, fifteen dollars for a prescription, and one hundred dollars per emergency room visit.

Making a person pay a little creates a small incentive for a person to only go to the emergency room when they actually need to. I never went to the emergency room if I knew that I could wait to see my own doctor.

About ten years ago, my ex-wife cut her hand. It was a deep and long cut, was bleeding profusely, and it obviously required stitches. Using my strict definition, it was an emergency. So, we went to the emergency room.

When we arrived, it was crowded. There were people sprawled everywhere. We signed in, showed the receptionist the bloody hand, and waited for our turn in the triage line.

After we had already been there for about two and a half hours, a young woman came in and approached the desk. She explained how she was having "another" migraine attack and she needed a shot to make it go away.

I was a migraine sufferer myself and I didn't even know such a thing existed. I suffered with migraines my entire life until I discovered on my own that they were caused by gluten intolerance. So I know about migraines.

As we sat there, attempting to keep pressure applied to the wound, this young lady sat directly across from us. She had brought a book with her which she began reading while she waited.

Reading a book? With a migraine? I became skeptical about her condition.

Everyone I knew, including myself, that ever had a migraine, would never even consider reading a book. That is the last thing I would do.

Then she got up, went to the vending machine and got a bag of chips. She quietly munched on them while engrossed in her book.

Now I am no doctor, but I can tell you that this woman most likely did not have a migraine. Ask anyone you know that truly has migraines, and they will tell you that eating while reading a book is not their preferred actions when experiencing a migraine. Most people want to climb into bed in a dark room.

So we sat for another 20 minutes. Then, the unthinkable happened. The women who was happily munching on her chips was called to be seen before us. At this point, we were there for about three hours and she was there for twenty minutes.

We got up and left the emergency room. We went to a local twenty-four hour pharmacy and bought extra sticky butterfly bandages. We went home and treated the wound ourselves. I haven't been to the emergency room since.

Many of the people in the emergency room will not be required to pay anything. So, for them, all they have to give is their time.

Liberals will tell us that if we make people pay a little, then they will never go to the emergency room. Well, many middle-class workers do not go to the emergency room anymore because their deductibles are so high that they can't afford it. Why don't they care about that?

For the low-income people who now receive totally free health care, there is no co-pay. Everything is free. For an illegal immigrant, they don't have to worry about paying because they are not actually part of the system. They are again breaking the law by not paying for this service, but hey, they've broken three or four now, so why not more? Breaking laws are a lot cheaper than following laws for an illegal immigrant.

The hospitals know this, so they have quietly passed these losses onto us, the responsible ones. The cost for us is the loss of affordable health care.

HMO's are all but gone. Hospital costs are through the roof. Co-pays are a thing of the past. Decent health care packages are replaced by high deductible insurance plans which is code words for catastrophic health insurance.

In other words, the only time the health insurance would actually pay your bill, is if your deductible has been met. But since these deductibles are anywhere from $3,000 to $10,000, most people will never even see their insurance pay anything unless they are admitted to the hospital or require expensive tests. Under these terrible plans, even your doctor visits aren't covered.

The old health plans used to incentivize us to make smart judgments about our health care. They incentivized us to utilize our doctors rather than use the emergency room as a doctor's office.

The new health plans, sadly, only incentivize us to not use the health care system at all.

It started deteriorating before Obamacare, but the decline culminated with Obamacare. The socialistic style of taxing the workers to pay for a free healthcare system just does not work in America.

The United States is by far the country that offers the most freedom. At the same time, we have the mightiest military in the world.

The might of the United States has kept the powers of evil at bay for 75 years. The United States liberated Europe in World War II and has been the defender of Europe ever since.

These European countries have enjoyed an alliance with the United States where the United States has acted as protector of the free world. As such, these countries are not encumbered by a military budget since the United States has always taken care of that for them. These European countries can then take the money that they have saved by not having a large military machine, and use that towards social programs like health care for all, as we, who are on the outside looking in at Europe, see a beautiful utopia.

Many on the left would love to make the United States into one of those European utopias. But who would defend us if we chose to divert all of our money to social programs? The unfortunate reality is, no one. There is no other power that can hold the forces of China, Russia, Iran, and many other bad regimes at bay. All we can do is constantly try to stay one step ahead militarily. Always maintain the strongest military in the world, and defend our freedoms and our way of life with force when required.

When the liberal politicians talk about the border, they most recently say that there should be no border. That everyone who wants to, regardless of background or intention, should just come into the United States unencumbered. That there should be no laws to keep anyone out, regardless of education, ability to contribute by maintaining a job, or malicious intent.

What about the politicians themselves? According to Roll Call, two-fifths of all Senators and Representatives are millionaires. That's about 214 millionaires out 535 members of Congress. It looks like there is money to be made in Congress.

You can bet that a lot of these congressmen and congresswomen are living in very nice homes. Homes that we will never be able to afford.

Contrary to popular reports that there are no walls around these homes, they actually all have walls. Interestingly, all homes have walls, and these walls keep out would be invaders. I'm relatively sure that Nancy Pelosi and Chuck Schumer don't keep the doors of their homes open for all to enter. I doubt that their pantries in their beautiful kitchens are made freely available for all to come and take what they are "entitled" to.

But these same types of liberals want outsiders of the United States, who aren't even citizens, to come and take from our pantries. Chuck and Nancy will never feel the pinch of living paycheck to paycheck. They are political hacks who have spent their entire careers duping their constituents into believing that they have their best interests in mind. They have quietly become millionaires, berating the top earners, all the while not letting on that they are the top earners.

Sadly, most of their constituents will never know the truth. Not because they aren't intelligent, but because they trust their politicians. They believe that these politicians really do have their wellbeing in mind. If this were true, then liberal politicians would be focusing on their legal constituents, not the illegal immigrants.

It reminds me of the story about the frog and the scorpion. A scorpion sees a frog by the riverside. The frog sees the scorpion and backs away. The scorpion asks the frog "Can you give me a ride across the river on your back?"

The frog responds, "If I did that, you would sting me."

The scorpion says, "Why would I sting you. Then we would both drown."

The frog sees the logic and takes the scorpion across the river on his back.

Halfway across the river, the scorpion stings the frog.

As they both slip beneath the water, the frog asks, "Why?"

The scorpion responds, "It's my nature."

And so it is with politics. The liberal constituents are the frog, and their not-so-trustworthy representatives are the scorpion. The constituents, believing in their representatives, think that their lives will be better. But while the constituents quietly keep waiting for things to improve, the representatives keep managing to get richer. It's not until it's too late that the constituents realize that they have been trusting the scorpions. It is the nature of liberal politicians to help their constituents a little, while benefiting themselves a lot.

Liberals and conservatives alike are guilty of this. But when looking at illegal immigration and how it affects the American worker, it is the liberals who are by far the greater offenders. If Chuck and Nancy had their way, there would be open borders and an infinite number of new Democrats pouring in. The country would collapse, the wages would drastically be suppressed, the American way of life would be gone, and only the rich would be immune.

Luckily for Chuck and Nancy, they fall into the category of the rich. So, while the rest of us are trying to combat crime and our own private economic collapse, Chuck and Nancy will be safely tucked away in their fancy homes with their fat bank accounts.

Fortunately, at least for the time being, this will not happen, because Hillary Clinton did not become president, and Donald Trump did.

The policies of Donald Trump for border security will save this country from its own demise. Building a wall, or at least having electronic security in place to act like a wall is essential. So, what is always baffling to me, are the arguments against the wall.

The first argument is that border crossings are significantly down. Therefore, a wall is not needed. But two years ago, border crossings were significantly up. So even if border crossings are currently low, they could just as easily increase to previous levels next week, next month, or next year. A wall prevents that from happening.

The second argument is that if the wall is used to stop drugs from coming across the border, then the drug cartels will just find other means, like more airplanes.

If you don't think about it much, this almost makes sense. But let's apply it to the home. A person lives in a second-floor apartment. There is a front door that opens to a hallway up to their apartment. The door has a window that keeps getting smashed by robbers who then gain entry into their home.

Now this person could do something about it. They could get a new reinforced door with no windows and build up the frame so that it can't be kicked in. But then, this person surmises, the robbers could just go and get a twenty-four foot ladder and put it against the outside wall of the house, climb up, break the window on the second floor to gain entry, and then carry out their robbery.

So, being the true liberal that he is, this person realizes that if he reinforces the door, the robbers could still find a way to get in. So, he does nothing but keep replacing his front door window.

In reality, doesn't it make sense to just reinforce the door? Sure, there may be other ways for the criminals to rob you, but those ways are much more difficult with a much higher risk of being caught. Most robbers won't bother.

So, for our second argument, why wouldn't we reinforce the border? There are other ways for people and drugs to get across, but those are much more difficult to accomplish and much easier to get caught. It would deter a very high percentage of illegals from even trying.

The United States has a porous, dangerous, undefended border. Previously, with President Obamas policies, anyone could get across. They could be child traffickers, terrorists, refugees, or just regular families trying to make a better life.

But that is exactly the point. We didn't know then, and we don't know how many are living among us right now, or what their true intentions are.

Thanks to the efforts of the Trump administration, the laws are finally being enforced, and the border is being protected the best as can be done under the circumstances. Hopefully, the left will wake up to the real threat of unwittingly letting people into our country who have not been properly vetted.

We know that not all illegal immigrants are criminals or terrorists, but we do know for a fact that some are. It's the ones who are criminals and terrorists that we have to worry about.

We cannot turn a blind eye to the threat of violent crime or terror just because we don't want to hurt someone's feelings, or just because we want to be altruistic in our ignorance. If we force everyone to come in legally, so that we can vet them properly, then we have a

much higher chance of not allowing in the people that
want to do us harm.

Immigrant vs. Illegal Immigrant

Valentina is a beautiful three-year-old girl. Her mom and dad came from Latin America. Unfortunately, her mom died when Valentina was born.

Now, the officer is putting handcuffs on her dad. Valentina is crying. She didn't do anything to deserve this. She is taken from her home and is placed in Child Care Services. She watches from the arms of a stranger as her dad is whisked into a police car and spirited away. It takes a few weeks, but Valentina is eventually reunited with other family members.

Valentina is a United States citizen. So is her dad. But her dad was arrested for armed robbery and will eventually spend time in prison. It is not Valentina's fault that her dad committed this crime, but she now has to spend years without him because he made the poor decision to break the law.

This is not a true story, but this type of scenario happens every day in the United States. Every single day, Americans commit crimes and eventually will go to prison. When this occurs, the American family will be torn apart. The children will be without one or both parents for years. This is as it should be. Criminals must be punished and removed from society to pay for their crime, to be rehabilitated, and to deter other people from committing crimes.

I have heard several liberal television panelists making the argument that children who are separated at the border from the illegal adults that are traveling with them is somehow horribly traumatic to these children. The children are then placed in Child Care Services until the adult that they travel with can be verified as being the parent or guardian. This separation can go on for weeks and in some cases months.

But wait a minute. The American families are separated for years. No one seems to care about that. Does anyone believe that the illegal immigrant children are more susceptible to the stress of separation than the American children? Of course not. It's a false argument to drive a narrative at the border in favor of illegal immigrants.

The fact is, a broken law is a broken law. If Americans are punished for breaking laws, then shouldn't illegal immigrants be punished as well? Does any American know of an American friend or family member that was convicted of a crime? On their way to jail, did the judge say that he didn't realize that the defendant had a child, therefore the defendant can go free? Of course not.

You may say that the illegal immigrant is only committing a misdemeanor, or the crime is just small compared to something like armed robbery, so they can't equate. But the issue isn't the crime, it's whether the children should be separated. In the case of armed robbery, the law clearly states that if convicted, the punishment by law is that you will go to jail and be separated from your child. The law also clearly states that if you enter or attempt to enter this country illegally and you are caught, then the punishment by law is that you are held or deported.

The previous administration allowed behavior such as the policy of catch and release, which allows adults and children, if caught, to be released immediately so that they can remain together and escape the law.

This seems like a good idea on paper, but in reality, it doesn't work. The adults are supposed to come back for a court hearing and they simply never do.

There are many illegals that take advantage of this. There have been cases where an adult with a child who enters illegally, is actually a human trafficker attempting to sell the child. So the latest court order that declares that the children must remain with the adult who brings them could in fact be leading the child into danger.

If we look at our American lawbreaker, they must post a bail to be released, if that is even an option. If the American doesn't show up for court, they will lose the bail and a warrant will be placed for their arrest. Eventually they would be caught and spend even more time in jail away from their children.

Doesn't it make more sense to put politics aside and do the intelligent thing? What is wrong with keeping the children separated from the adults until the adult can be fully vetted and proven to be the parent or guardian?

American parents who commit crimes are separated from their children for years. There are no talking head psychologists lamenting the poor plight of the American children. Yet these same psychologists are bemoaning the poor illegal immigrant children and how the relatively short time that they are separated from their guardians will cause irreparable damage to their tender psyches.

The truth is, that even when they are being detained, the children are experiencing vastly superior conditions compared to where they came from. It is sad that they are separated from their parents or guardians because their parents or guardians chose to break the law, but that is the case for all families. Not only illegal immigrants.

However, just because it is sad, does not make it wrong. Just like the Americans in the United States, if you don't want to be separated from your children, then don't break the law.

Another thing about the immigration argument that really gets my blood pressure up is the way that the left and some other individuals conflate, or intentionally confuse the term immigrant with illegal immigrant. Let's not be fooled by this political ploy. An immigrant is a person who came to this country legally. An ***illegal*** immigrant is a person who entered the country illegally, thereby breaking the laws that Congress have enacted to keep our borders safe and secure. Therefore, by definition, these illegal immigrants have already broken the law the second they step across our border.

Remember this when anyone from Congress complains about or ridicules the current immigration laws, whether Republican or Democrat, Representative or Senator, they are the ones who created these laws. When you hear Chuck Schumer or Nancy Pelosi lamenting over the plight of the illegal immigrants at the southern border, just remember that it is they who have the power to change it.

They can point the finger at the President, and deflect the blame by loudly proclaiming that the President has the power to write executive orders and that is how the immigration law should be dealt with, but Congress is the maker of laws. If a law, over time, is deemed to be incorrect and must be updated or eliminated, it is *only* Congress who has the power to make, change, or eliminate a law. The President can, like a dictator, issue executive orders to shunt Congress. In most cases, Congress detests these executive orders since it is a back-door method to go around Congress and make things happen without their approval.

At any other time, the liberals would be decrying President Trumps use of executive orders, but in the case of illegal immigrants, it is politically expedient to blame the laws that Congress enacted on President Trump. So the left now decries the fact that President Trump is *not* issuing executive orders.

During the Obama years, the Democrats had full control of both houses of Congress and elected to do nothing with regards to immigration reform.

In 2010, President Obama's base was demanding that he implement immigration reforms without congressional approval.

In October of 2010, President Obama said "I am not King. I can't do these things just by myself."

In March of 2011, President Obama said "with respect to the notion that I can just suspend deportations through executive order, that's just not the case."

In May of 2011, President Obama said that he couldn't "just bypass Congress and change the law myself. That's not how democracy works."

In 2012, President Obama completely contradicted himself and decided to go around Congress and the Constitution of the United States after all, signing an Executive Order to create DACA, the Deferred Action for Childhood Arrivals program. This program basically allows children of illegal immigrants the ability to obtain work permits without the fear of being deported.

Most people do not consider this a bad thing, but it should have gone through Congress. President Trump attempted to force Congress to act on this by allowing the time limit imposed in President Obama's executive order to expire, but a liberal judge prevented it from expiring.

It is interesting to note that in this case DACA is not a law. It is simply an executive order that does not have the authority or approval of Congress, the government body actually make the laws. Therefore, the judge, whose job is to interpret the law, actually created his own law by not allowing the executive order to expire.

Liberal judges are doing this on a regular basis, especially when it comes to the policies of President Trump. These "activist judges", rather than interpret the law, make decisions that create new laws that must be enforced because of the power of the court. These rulings cannot be ignored and must be complied to until a higher court reverses the ruling. This is one more method that the liberal left uses to usurp the power of the people.

It is widely accepted most people that immigration is a very important tool that the United States has always used. We would not have come as far as we have without it. When the country began booming during the industrial revolution, there would never have been enough workers and entrepreneurs to push the country towards being the greatest country on earth were it not for legal immigrants.

Unfortunately, the sad truth is that most of the highly educated immigrant candidates are already in line to enter the United States legally. They are spending thousands of dollars, submitting forms, and taking years to finally gain legal entry into the United States.

These potential legal immigrants truly aspire to be American. They are happy to assimilate into the United States while still maintaining their heritage. More importantly, they do not scoff at our immigration laws. They follow our laws. They submit their forms. They pay their fees, and eventually, they become legal citizens.

This brings up one extremely important point about immigration. It doesn't take a genius to decipher that liberals want illegal immigrants to enter the United States so that they can bolster the numbers in their voting bloc. If twenty million Illegal Immigrants were given amnesty tomorrow, you can bet that there would be twenty million new votes for the Democratic Party.

Poppycock! Say the Democrats. Their only interest is in the health and well-being of these poor illegal immigrants is what they proclaim. They have no interest in allowing illegal immigrants to vote, they declare. Besides, they assert, illegals can't vote, right?

Not so fast. If I were a Democrat (shudder), I would begin a process of getting illegals the rights of American citizens. No one is going to allow full citizenship status. So what I would do is start with baby steps. You know, let illegal immigrants get simple things like drivers licenses first. Then I would push to allow them some simple voting rights. Something like voting for the local school board. These are elected officials, but it's at the local level, so no one would notice.

From there, I would move to city wide elections, where I could now have precedent to claim state wide voting rights for the non-citizens. Once statewide voting rights were procured, I would create a case to allow voting rights for federal elections.

Preposterous! You say? Well, in October of 2013, Governor Jerry Brown of California did sign into law the ability for illegal immigrants the right to obtain drivers licenses starting in 2015.

First step of illegal immigrant voting plan...check.

Now the illegal immigrants have a license from the state that is one step towards removing their illegal status. It also makes it much easier to commit voter fraud. Even though they are not technically allowed to vote in state and federal elections, there is an automatic voter registration process that Governor Brown implemented to "increase voter turnout". The claim is that there are "safeguards" in place to prevent non-citizens from registering.

Many of the liberal constituents, before this law, routinely commit voter fraud. There are plenty of stories over the past several years of one person voting multiple times, or one person voting in multiple states, or dead people voting. These illegal votes are almost always for the Democrats.

You may not have heard about these incidents. If you get your nightly news from the big three liberal networks, then you will not have heard about them. Obviously, it does not help the liberal agenda to report that the Democrats are cheating in the elections, so the liberal networks don't report these stories.

So, voter fraud is happening. That is why the liberals fight so hard to stop proof of voter registration by showing identification at the voting booth. Their claim is that poor people are not smart enough to figure out how to get the voter ID, so they won't bother to go and vote.

Isn't it interesting that California has figured out a way to get millions of illegal immigrants into their voter registration system, but they then claim that they cannot do the same for American citizens? Another false argument that is used to keep the conservative voice in California silenced.

Meanwhile, in San Francisco, California, the local government has passed a law in November of 2016 that will allow illegal immigrants to vote in local school board elections.

Second step of illegal immigrant voting plan...check.

The justification is that since the illegal immigrants have children in school, then they should have a say in how the school system is run.

Why should they? The illegal immigrant parents chose to come here against our laws, so we now reward them with a voice in our local government? San Francisco apparently doesn't care about the law, or its citizens.

Each illegal that votes is negating the vote of one American citizen, but San Francisco is ok with that because the illegal immigrant will almost surely vote in favor of liberal principles. Since the vote that is negated will more than likely be conservative, then all is well with the San Francisco government.

People of San Francisco, wake up! The illegal immigrants have broken the law. I agree that the kids should not be held responsible for their parents, but why on earth would you want to reward their parents, who broke the law, by now giving them rights to vote in your local government?

That is only a rhetorical question. I already know the answer, which is that the government officials want to remain in power so that they can keep the money and power flowing. It is all about votes and money, hidden behind altruistic lies, to keep the Democrats in power.

But, why would *any* American citizen want to allow an immigrant who has entered illegally to stay? This, when looked at objectively is obvious, isn't it? We have laws for a reason. We have border laws to prevent non-US citizens from entering our country and using up our valuable resources.

If an illegal immigrant is utilizing welfare of *any* kind, then that is an amount of welfare, be it food stamps, housing, education, healthcare, or monetary funds that is no longer available to US citizens. The liberals will talk about "poverty" in the United States, and how we need more tax revenue to combat it. But isn't it a no-brainer, that the first step to combating American poverty is to actually give the American resources to the Americans?

Think of the millions of illegal immigrants who are receiving some form of public assistance. For every one of those illegal immigrants, one more American citizen could have been cared for. I wonder how many liberals who are actually in a lower income bracket and don't qualify for assistance, realize that they are foregoing potential public assistance so that an illegal immigrant can enjoy the benefits ahead of them. Actual American citizens lose out to illegal immigrants who qualify before them.

Liberals will of course claim that this is not the case. That the resources are there for all Americans and that the resources are somehow unlimited so that all Americans have access to these unlimited resources. Any of us who know or knew someone who may have needed public assistance realizes that this is not true. If you need housing because of your low income level, then you get on a list and wait in line. Be assured that the line is now filled with illegal immigrants ahead of you. Also, be assured that many of the apartments that are already taken will be happily occupied by illegal immigrants.

Ultimately, the non-working illegal immigrants are living as well, or sometimes better than the hard-working Americans who are just above the eligibility threshold. These illegal immigrants are sucking up resources that can no longer be used for the hard-working Americans.

The same is true for pay. Illegal immigrants generally work for less than Americans. Thereby creating the old liberal standard, "Illegals come here to do the work that Americans don't want to do". They leave out the end of the sentence, which is "Illegals come here to do the work that Americans don't want to do because the pay is too low".

The "need" for illegal immigrants then becomes a self-fulfilling prophecy by the left. The poor liberal decisions weaken the economy and lowers the wages for many of these jobs. The illegal immigrants are happy to come in and get paid less, which is many times the wages they can earn in their home countries. The gain of the illegal immigrant in the United States is the loss of the American worker.

I understand that most illegals are only coming to try and make a better life for themselves and their children. But so are the legal immigrants. They have the same purpose, except they do it legally.

So, why do we need to ensure immigrants are legal anyway? That has a simple answer. We must totally understand the intentions of anyone who enters our country. There are many bad people in the world who would love to get across our borders to do harm. There are also many uneducated people who would like to come to the United States to take advantage of the welfare system... and millions of illegal immigrants do just that.

Still, this is the least of the problems. There are many illegal immigrants who come to this country and commit crimes such as rape, theft, and murder. It may be a small minority, but tell that to the Americans who have lost love ones because an illegal immigrant was driving drunk or an illegal immigrant murdered their child.

The usual political ploy from the left is that only a very small percentage of illegal immigrants commit crimes. In fact, the crime rate of illegal immigrants is lower than for American citizens they will proudly proclaim.

The crime rate statistic is questionable since sanctuary cities routinely release illegal immigrants who commit crimes without actually ever charging them. But even if we put that aside, who cares about the crime statistic? Do the parents and family of Kate Steinle or the parents and family of Molly Tibbetts, two beautiful young women who were murdered by illegal immigrants, really care about the statistics? Do all of the parents and family of all the unfortunate victims of illegal immigrants really care that the crime rate among illegals might be less than American citizens?

I know *I* don't care. If you approach it logically, there is one gigantic difference between an illegal immigrant who commits a heinous crime and an American citizen who commits a heinous crime. The difference being that the illegal immigrant did not have to be here, thereby making the murder or other violent crime totally preventable.

If an American citizen decides to commit a murder, or drive drunk and get into an accident, or commit any other type of crime, there is nothing we can do about it until after it happens. Usually, the offender is caught and put behind bars, where they belong.

Illegal immigrants should not be here in the first place. If the government was doing their job correctly, these illegal immigrants would never enter the country. Thus, Kate Steinle and Molly Tibbetts would still be alive.

We can pretend that there was nothing we could do, but the sad truth is that any crime perpetrated by an illegal immigrant is a crime that could have been prevented. If an illegal immigrant decides to commit a murder, drive drunk, or commit any other serious crimes, then the results of that crime can be placed squarely on the shoulders of the politicians who allow the illegals into the country and then allow them to stay. In almost all cases of violent illegal immigrant crime against American citizens recently, the offending illegal immigrant was deported several times. Our laws are so lax, that the illegal immigrant laughs at our immigration system as they are dropped off in their home country, where they promptly turn around and walk right back into the United States again illegally.

The United States helps many, many countries every year in the form of financial aid. Billions and billions of dollars. That is how we help the unfortunate people in other countries. We cannot just allow uneducated, non-contributors, and criminals into the country to become lifelong users of our welfare system and violate our laws. It seems cold and uncaring, but if we let everyone in with no limitations, regardless of their background or their ability to support themselves, then the United States would quickly become just like the third world countries that the illegals came from.

We can have a kind heart, and give aid to these countries, but we can't trade our citizens, our livelihood, our safety, and our security to open the borders and allow everyone to come flooding in. By placing illegal immigrants above American citizens, the left is slowly changing the country into a model that is not sustainable.

Over the last presidency, it has become politically incorrect to believe that Americans should come first in the United States. It is this far left attitude that has partially created the environment where someone like Donald Trump could even become president.

Thankfully, the current presidency is reminding all of us of what it means to be American. We should all take pride in our country and our countrymen. We should all take pride in a robust, safe, and secure legal immigration policy. We should all take pride in putting a strong foot forward on the world stage and becoming the world leader that America should be.

Having peace on earth where all men and women are equal is a lofty goal, but with the current state of world affairs, it is only a foolish dream. There are too many other countries who do not think the way we do.

There are more than a few countries who would destroy the United States and our allies in a nuclear second if they could. The best thing we can do is to be vigilant, and maintain a strong and safe border to ensure that we keep out the bad people who want to do us harm.

The Collusion Delusion

The left has been working very, very hard to discredit Donald Trump, his presidency, and the people around him. The main goal is to regain control of the Congress and to impeach President Trump by any means possible. Those means, when analyzed logically, only prove to be a plethora of baseless claims, wild accusations, unfounded theories, illogical reasoning, and innuendos designed to discredit this president for power and political gain. Let's take a look at some of the "evidence" that the left purports to back their claims of Russian ties and obstruction of justice.

Trump Tower Meeting

Attendees:

Donald Trump Jr. - Donald Trump's son

Paul Manafort

> Donald Trump's Campaign Manager at the time of the meeting

Jared Kushner

> Donald Trump's son-in-law and Senior Advisor

Natalia Veselnitskaya

> Russian Lawyer

Bob Goldstone

> British Music Publicist

Rinat Akhmetshin

Russian-American Lobbyist

Anatoli Samachornov

Russian Translator

Irakly Kaveadze

VP of Aras Agalarov's real estate company. Agalarov is a wealthy Russian real estate developer

Liberal Argument: The meeting was an attempt by the Trump Campaign to get damaging information on Hillary Clinton to use in the presidential campaign to discredit her.

Facts:

- Acquiring truthful but damaging information against a political opponent is not against the law
- Meeting with Russians is not against the law
- There was never any information exchanged
- Jared Kushner realized that the Hillary Clinton information was a ruse by the Russian's to make the meeting happen. Ten minutes into the meeting, he texted his assistant and asked that he call him so that he could have an excuse to politely leave the meeting, and he did.
-

Although the meeting appears to have been an actual attempt to get information on the Clinton campaign, no information was ever presented by the Russians. Also, there was never any follow up by the Trump campaign, which would make sense since the meeting was requested by the Russians under false pretenses.

The left has characterized this meeting as something that is illegal. However, how can they criticize this simple meeting, where nothing was exchanged, and then not investigate the Trump Dossier, where false information was actually paid for by the DNC and the Clinton Campaign? The information in this dossier, which has been proven false, was actually paid for by the Democratic National Committee and the Hillary Clinton Campaign. Money was exchanged by the DNC and the Clinton Campaign in order to acquire damaging information about the Trump Campaign.

The left is furious over a simple meeting by the Trump team, where no information was exchanged, and no money was exchanged, but they are totally complacent about false information that was actually purchased by the Clinton Campaign. This totally, demonstrably false dossier was ultimately used by the FBI to get a FISA warrant so that they could spy on the Trump Campaign.

Since the source of many of these false claims were Russian nationals, that means that the Clinton Campaign paid the Russians to generate lies about the Trump Campaign so the FBI could use this false information as an excuse to spy on the Trump Campaign, and then leak the information back to the Clinton Campaign. If you made this convoluted plot up in a spy novel, no one would believe it.

Another interesting note, is that the latest focus on this meeting by the liberals is: "What did Donald Trump know about the meeting, and when did he know it?"

This is all that is left for the Democrats. There is no substance to the meeting itself. No information exchanged. No money exchanged. Nothing illegal happened. So, all the Democrats have left is to attempt to find a misstatement and then claim that it's a lie. As if the lie will validate the supposed collusion.

That is the infamous "perjury trap" that everyone that is being investigated must continually worry about. If the investigators can't find any real crime or anything of substance to continue the investigation, then they pour over television appearances, interviews, tweets, and other documents, and then ask questions that they already know the answers to. The entire process is a long, drawn out interrogation to make you say two statements that seemingly contradict each other, and now you're a liar. The conclusion, since you "lied" about that, then you must be lying about everything.

The perjury trap is the pathetic death throes of what should be a valid investigation. If you look hard enough and long enough, you will find contradictory statements from everyone.

Obstruction of Justice

When James Comey, the Director of the FBI, was fired by President Trump on May 9, 2017, the Democrats were furious and started screaming "obstruction of justice". One can easily see how firing a person who might be investigating you could be a form of obstruction of justice. But let's not look at it from such a high level. Let's dig a little deeper.

What kind of FBI Director did President Trump inherit when he became President in 2017?

In James Comey, President Trump inherited an FBI Director that already had a storied past. Comey liked the spotlight. He liked holding press conferences to give updates on the Hillary Clinton investigation. He did not mind going around his supervisor, Attorney General Loretta Lynch, and making his own decisions. He didn't trust his superiors. He felt he was endowed with a higher purpose, and that as such, he could be investigator, judge, and jury.

The events that led up to the general election was an FBI circus with Comey as the ringleader. His falsely altruistic principles made him an equal opportunity player. Raining his decrees down on Republicans and Democrats alike.

When he disparaged the Republicans, the Republicans hated him and the Democrats loved him. When he disparaged the Democrats, the Democrats hated him and the Republicans loved him. The entire time, Comey standing tall and looking down at the ignorant and unknowing masses.

When President Trump took office, he did what he always does. He gave Comey a chance.

Comey took that chance and started the Russian Interference investigation. President Trump watched as Comey quickly began investigating people with ties to Trump. Comey testified that on at least three occasions, he told President Trump that he was not under investigation.

Now put yourself in Donald Trump's shoes. Rod Rosenstein presents a recommendation to fire James Comey based on his actions during the presidential campaign. Everyone agrees that Comey did not handle this period of time in a way that a Director of the FBI should have handled it, and to top it off, you know that the Russian Collusion angle is nonsense.

So, what do you do? Do you allow an important position like the Director of the FBI be held by a completely incompetent, inept, narcissistic person like James Comey, or do you fire him? I would fire him.

The left's argument at this point is, since James Comey is leading the Russian Collusion investigation against Donald Trump, then he should be untouchable. Except that, by Comey's own statements, Donald Trump was not being investigated.

Comey worked for President Trump. As soon as Trump saw that Comey was incapable of directing the FBI, Trump had to let him go.

Then, as if to validate Trump's decision, on his way out Comey leaked FBI information to a friend of his. This leaked information was the basis for justifying a Special Counsel. Comey testified that he purposely leaked this information to cause a Special Counsel to be called.

The head of the FBI leaked FBI information. That's all you need to know about James Comey.

Firings, Demotions, and Sudden Departures

Since the Russian Investigation has begun, there has also been a less publicized background investigation going on. This investigation is related to how and why the Russian investigation started.

There are a number of people that have been involved with getting the collusion narrative off the ground and into the thoughts and minds of everyday Americans. Many of these people have been demoted, fired, or quit on their own in light of the scandal that is unfolding. Here are a few, including many high-ranking officials:

1. James Comey – Director of the FBI - Fired on May 9, 2017 by President Donald Trump. Some believe that his handling of the Russia investigation had something to do with it. Since this investigation was being run like Comey's previous investigations, that is to say ineptly, then I personally believe he was fired for good reason.

2. Sally Yates – Deputy Attorney General – A holdover from the Obama Administration, Yates was fired for insubordination after she refused to defend President Trump's executive order on illegal immigration.

3. Andrew McCabe – Deputy Director of the FBI - Fired for lack of candor. McCabe also had a huge conflict of interest, since he was investigating the Hillary Clinton email Probe while his wife was running for public office in Virginia using donated funds from a friend of Hillary Clinton.

4. Peter Kadzik – Department of Justice liaison to Congress, Assistant Attorney General for Legislative Affairs during the Obama

Administration – Departed after alleged conflict of interest with Clinton Campaign and leaking.

5. Peter Strzok – FBI Counterintelligence Expert – Fired over his obvious bias towards the Donald Trump presidency. His arrogance when questioned by the House Judiciary and House Oversight Committees was palpable. His disdain for President Trump was obvious and disgusting. It seems unbelievable that someone with that much bias would be allowed to participate in an investigation on the very person he personally loathed. One of the most egregious texts made by Strzok was reported by Breitbart.

Page asked Strzok: "[Trump's] not ever going to become president right? Right?!" – to which he responded "No. No he won't. We'll stop it."

It appears he did try to stop it. Peter Strzok was in charge of the investigation into Anthony Weiner's laptop. Initially, it was confiscated for sexting charges with a minor, but it was later discovered that there was classified information on the laptop from Wiener's wife, Huma Abedin, who was Hillary Clinton's aide. Strzok held onto this information for a month in September of 2016, which appears to be an attempt to keep the information quiet until after the general election.

6. Lisa Page – FBI Attorney – Resigned amidst the texting scandal between her and her apparent lover, Peter Strzok.

7. James Baker – Top FBI Attorney – Baker retired after being reassigned by the new Director of the FBI, Christopher Wray. Baker was investigated for sharing classified information with reporters, but has not been charged with anything.

8. Bruce Ohr - Associate Deputy Attorney General – Demoted after the Trump Administration Department of Justice discovered his ties to Peter Strzok and Christopher Steel in regards to pushing the Trump Dossier. Ohr told lawmakers that he had a conflict of interest because his wife worked at the opposition research firm, Fusion GPS, at the same time as Christopher Steele. Fusion GPS is the firm that helped create the Trump Dossier. Interestingly, Ohr was allowed to remain on the investigation even though there was an obvious conflict of interest.

These names are not the complete list and more seem to be added almost every week. It is obvious to even the casual reader that there was something nefarious going on at the Obama Department of Justice.

Nearly every name above has substantial evidence indicating that they were operating with bias against Donald Trump.

Yet, Robert Mueller, who is heading the Russian Interference investigation, has never interviewed Bruce Ohr. The man who was the liaison between his own wife, Christopher Steele, Fusion GPS, and Peter Strzok, and who was instrumental in pushing the Trump Dossier forward, was never interviewed by the Mueller team?

How can that be? How can one of the most pivotal characters in this scheme not even get contacted?

The obvious, glaring answer, is that the Mueller team has no interest in finding the truth. Their only interest is to find something to discredit President Trump.

Just recently, it has come to light that the Mueller team wants to speak with President Trump, but only if he is under oath. The liberals will claim that if he has nothing to worry about, then why shouldn't he be under oath?

Once again, in stark contrast to how Donald Trump gets treated compared to Hillary Clinton, Clinton was interviewed by the FBI. No notes were taken, no video, no audio, and she was not under oath.

The unfairness and hypocrisy are blatantly obvious, but the media is the voice of the liberal left, so most Americans will never see or hear the evidence of this injustice, nor will they ever learn the truth about Mueller's team.

Robert Mueller, if he is the brilliant prosecutor that we are all led to believe, would certainly understand the concept of perception. In any investigation, the perception, through actions, must always show the citizens that the investigation is fair, unbiased, and just.

If Mueller wanted to ensure that his team, which is investigating a Republican president, gave a correct perception of fairness, then surely, he would fill his team with Republicans, Democrats, and Independents. Let's take a look at his team.

Mueller released the below names of lawyers on his team. According to Business Insider and The Daily Caller, they are:

Michael Dreeben – Registered Democrat - the deputy solicitor general overseeing the Department of Justice's criminal docket.

Andrew Weissmann – Registered Democrat - joined Mueller's team after taking a leave of absence from his current job leading the DOJ's criminal fraud unit.

Jeannie Rhee – Registered Democrat - resigned from the WilmerHale law firm to join Mueller's investigation.

James Quarles – Registered Democrat - resigned from the WilmerHale law firm to join Mueller's investigation.

Aaron Zebley – No Party Affiliation - longtime FBI staffer who spent years in the counterterrorism division as a special agent before becoming the agency's chief of staff under Mueller's former leadership.

Greg Andres – Registered Democrat - joined the investigation on August 1, adding expertise in foreign bribery to Mueller's team.

Zainab Ahmad – No Party Affiliation - best known for her counterterrorism experience as an assistant US attorney in the Eastern District of New York.

Aaron Zelinsky – Registered Democrat - came to the Mueller probe in June after a three-year stint in the US attorney's office in Maryland, where he worked under Rod Rosenstein, who is now the deputy attorney general with authority over the Trump-Russia investigation.

Kyle Freeny – Registered Democrat - joined Mueller's team shortly after withdrawing from the Justice Department. Political donations of $250 donations to each of Obama's presidential campaigns, and $250 to Hillary Clinton's 2016 campaign, according to Politico.

Andrew Goldstein – Registered Democrat - before joining the Mueller probe, Goldstein led the public corruption unit in the US Attorney's office in the Southern District of New York, where he worked under Preet Bharara, the federal prosecutor who was famously fired by Trump in March after refusing to resign.

Elizabeth Prelogar – Registered Democrat - a lawyer on loan to the Mueller probe from the US solicitor general's office. Prelogar is fluent in Russian.

Brandon Van Grack – Registered Democrat - worked in the US Attorney's office for the Eastern District of Virginia, where he helped prosecute national security, espionage, and international crime cases.

Adam Jed – Registered Democrat - the only lawyer on Mueller's team to have never worked as a prosecutor, according to The Daily Beast. Instead, Jed has experience as an appellate lawyer in the Justice Department's civil division.

Scott Meisler – No Party Affiliation - worked mostly in the Justice Department's criminal division since 2009 as an appellate lawyer.

Rush Atkinson – Registered Democrat - a trial attorney for more than four years in the Securities and Financial Fraud Unit of the Justice Department's criminal division.

Brian Richardson – No Party Affiliation - joined Mueller's team in July 2017, shortly after clerking for Supreme Court Justice Stephen Breyer.

Ryan Dickey – Registered Democrat - joined Mueller's team in November 2017, after working for years as an assistant US attorney in the Eastern District of Virginia

Uzo Asonye – Registered Democrat - an assistant US attorney with experience prosecuting embezzlement and bribery cases.

Of the eighteen names of people who are or were on Mueller's team, fourteen are Democrats, four have no party affiliation, and zero are Republican.

Stated another way, the political makeup of Mueller's team is:

77.8% Democrat
22.2% no affiliation
0% Republican.

Zero Republicans? This fact alone should make us all wonder about the real intentions of the Russia investigation. Why would Mueller load it with Democrats and no Republicans, if not to skew the results? Even if Mueller did not plan to do this, how could he not see the perception this would create and the dark cloud that would then hang over any results, especially if the results favored Democrats?

Even more important now, is that the makeup of his team being primarily Democrat with no Republicans, intentional or not, has come to light. So why doesn't he correct it?

Either he is so arrogant, that like Comey, he believes he knows what is right and wrong more than all of us who are beneath him, or he really does want to slant his team to the left. Either way, it should be unacceptable.

Liberal's argue that since Mueller is a registered Republican, then the political makeup is now no longer valid. I would argue that absolute power corrupts absolutely, and the power that Mueller has with his objective of finding something on Trump, supersedes his party affiliation. Also, Mueller has a history with, and is friends of James Comey, who Trump fired.

Wait! You exclaim. How can the friend, and former boss of James Comey, who is a central figure in the Russian Investigation, not be biased with a conflict of interest?

Obviously, he can't. Another ridiculous reality of the Russian Investigation. The two men who have the most control over the investigation, Robert Mueller and Rod Rosenstein, have blatant conflicts of interest.

Mueller's ties to James Comey, who should be a witness in this investigation, should automatically force Mueller to recuse himself. Rosenstein's ties to Comey, because he was the one who recommended Comey's firing, makes Rosenstein a witness as well. This fact should force Rosenstein to recuse himself just as Jeff Sessions did.

I can understand why President Trump is upset at Attorney General Jeff Sessions for recusing himself from the investigation. After all, Trump wants someone like Sessions leading the investigation who is fair.

However, Sessions' actions actually prove that he is the *only* one that is fair and unbiased. His minimal and legal contact with the Russian diplomats was never really a conflict.

But Sessions, who has true integrity and character, recused himself from the case. Meanwhile, Mueller and Rosenstein, who both have obvious and blatant conflicts of interest, refuse to recuse themselves.

This is just further proof of how biased and unjust this investigation is. The men leading this investigation refuse to apply fairness.

Hillary Clinton was given a pass, and all the people who could testify against her were given immunity (see Investigating the Investigators). There is substantial, real evidence that should be followed up in regards to the Clinton Email Investigation, Fusion GPS, Benghazi, The Uranium Deal, The Clinton Foundation, the list seems endless.

Donald Trump, on the other hand, is endlessly investigated. The people that surround him are spied on and investigated as far back as their records exist.

The crimes that the four Americans committed, who were related to Trump, were all convicted of crimes that had nothing to with Donald Trump or his campaign.

Yet, the investigation goes on, and on, and on.

It seems, that the only way to get to the bottom of all of this bias, is to investigate the investigators and bring everything into the light.

Investigating the Investigators

Once upon a time, there was a Special Prosecutor that was charged with finding information about a crime that was potentially committed by the President of the United States. Like any good prosecutor, he dug and dug. He called in witnesses and he called in possible cohorts. He sifted, parsed, and perused the mountains of information. He followed leads that went far astray from the main objective.

But no matter how hard he tried, he could not find any evidence of a real crime from the President of the United States. He questioned people who worked with the President. He questioned people who dealt with the President. He questioned friends of the President. He questioned the family of the President.

During the very long and expensive investigation, the Special Prosecutor uncovered that one of the witnesses had ties to illegal loans. *Now* the Special Prosecutor knew he had his leverage. He would threaten the man with jail time. Of course, the man was not the real target of the investigation. He was just a pawn in the Special Prosecutor's game of chess.

But the chess game was really no game after all. People's lives would be destroyed for insignificant misstatements or perhaps small insignificant lies.

It is interesting to note that politicians, the people who create the laws, actually lie all the time. Today they will tell you one thing and tomorrow it will be totally different. The third day will back to the first thing. Citizens could never do this, but it is ok when politicians do it.

Our man, as it turns out, pleads guilty to felony counts, in exchange of course, for testimony about the president.

Meanwhile, our Special Prosecutor is constantly trying to get our President to come in for an "interview". He assures the President that he is not a target, and that he only wants to ask some questions for clarification.

The President is leery, however, sensing that the Special Prosecutor is really just attempting to set a perjury trap. After all, if someone is questioned long enough, with the same questions being asked in various ways, they will eventually contradict themselves. And.... BINGO... another liar headed for the slammer.

Finally, our President agrees to be interviewed, makes a few memorable statements, and gets through virtually unscathed.

Oh wait! You thought I was talking about President Trump? No, no. I was talking about President Clinton!

My point related to President Trump, is that whether it's Democrats or Republicans doing the prosecuting, Special Prosecutors feel like they must find something. Anything.

As the days, weeks, and months go by, and they find nothing, there is a need to justify the time and expenditure. They find small fish who are somehow related to the President, and go over their lives, finances, and history with a fine-tooth comb. If they dig deep enough and long enough, they *will* find something.

How many people have committed a crime without ever even realizing it? There are thousands of laws. It would be very easy to commit a crime without knowing it. Especially crimes related to finance. If you have a lot of wealth, businesses, and property, there are just too many laws that must thoroughly be understood. If you make one mistake, then there it will sit, waiting for some special prosecutor to discover it someday and help you find your way to state prison.

In the end, it's never about the initial investigation. The threads begin to spread out from the center. Next thing you know, the special prosecutor is investigating lying on loan applications, or lying about having an affair, or trying to turn legally paid non-disclosure agreements into a crime.

So why does the Trump investigation stray so far from the initial investigation, which was Russian interference in the 2016 elections? Let me paraphrase Dan Bongino, a frequent guest on FOX News, who said it best. "The Mueller investigation should be a crime in search of the person who committed it. Instead, it is an investigation of a person, Donald Trump, in search of a crime."

The crime started with Russian interference and quickly spread to collusion with the Russians by the Trump campaign. Not one shred of collusion evidence has ever been offered, other than a totally fake dossier that was discredited long ago. The FBI, under the leadership of James Comey, allowed this phony, unsubstantiated document to be used as evidence to justify spying on the Trump campaign.

Let that sink in a bit. A fabricated document, which was proven to be paid for by the Hillary Clinton campaign, was used as justification to issue a FISA warrant, which allows wiretapping of the Trump Campaign, which is the opposition party to Hillary Clinton.

Richard Nixon would have been envious of the reach that the Clinton Campaign has. To be able to manipulate the Justice Department is mind boggling. To call Hillary Clinton out in public and then have the Justice Department cover it up is downright criminal.

The liberals believe that Mueller is sitting on a mountain of evidence against President Trump. So far, there have been several indictments of Russian Nationals from Special Prosecutor Mueller, but they went out of their way to say that there no Americans knowingly involved. Everyone else who was indicted or persecuted, um, I mean prosecuted, were done so on charges totally unrelated to Donald Trump or the Russians. The indictments include General Michael Flynn, who lied to the investigators. George Papadopoulos, who lied to investigators. Paul Manafort, who had tax issues, and Michael Cohen for tax and bank fraud.

Flynn and Papadopoulos gave in right away. Manafort fought it but was ultimately convicted. Cohen tried to fight, but the prospect of the investigators possibly implicating his family or the prospect of his assets being seized by investigators were evidently just too much, and he too gave in to the unlimited power of the state. Pleading down from 65 years to 3-5 years in return for a vague statement to implicate Donald Trump in an attempt to turn his legally paid non-disclosure agreement into a crime.

The idea that a government official can threaten you and your family with prison time or by seizing your assets is a frightening prospect. The philosophy being that you will succumb to the threats and in return for immunity from prosecution, tell all the nasty, criminal activities of someone higher up on the criminal food chain. Allen Dershowitz, a Constitutional Attorney and Scholar who was a Professor at Harvard Law School, describes this action of squeezing a person to make them give you information on the criminal activities of another person as not only making them "sing", but possibly make them "compose".

If a person's livelihood, or freedom, or family's financial wellbeing, or their family in general is at risk, then they will do whatever it takes to keep themselves out of jail and to keep their family's security safe. They will do whatever it takes. So, if they must embellish a few stories, or make up a few events to ensure the security of their family, then that is what they will do.

Let's approach this from a different point of view.

It is a well-known fact that American prisoner of war have been beaten and tortured during various wars in an attempt for the other side to get information, or to get a confession. This "confession" would be in the form of the prisoner agreeing that what the United States was doing was wrong, and that their government was correct, America is bad, their government is good, etc. All for propaganda purposes.

Most prisoners of war eventually give the "confession", some after many beatings and broken bones. Back home in America, we see the "confessions" on television, and we all know the confessions were coerced and had no meaning.

This only proves that every man has a breaking point. If a man is tortured long enough, he will tell his captors what they want to hear to make the torture stop.

But aren't the tactics used by Mueller and his ilk the same tactics but to a much lesser degree?

Before the liberals start chastising me for daring to equate American war heroes to Paul Manafort, let me clarify that I am not equating these men at all. I am equating the torture of prisoners of war to the tactic of systematically destroying a man to make him say what the investigators want to hear.

In a POW scenario, the captors are systematically and psychologically destroying a man's will through mental and physical torture. The alternatives are to comply and confess, or continue with the unrelenting torture.

In a criminal scenario, the prosecutor uses a form of psychological torture by outlining what will happen to the defendant and his family if they do not comply, and come up with the information that the investigator wants to hear. Who can deny that essentially threatening life in prison, or financial ruin to you or your family is not a form of psychological torture?

The scenarios are vastly different, but the results are the same. Tell me what I want to hear or you will suffer horrible consequences.

Most of these people have done something, knowingly or not, that is a felony. If they can negotiate a deal to keep themselves or their family secure, then they will.

I can envision the logic of their thinking as the investigators interrogate them, explain the dire consequences of what will happen to them and their families, and then dangle immunity over their heads if they come up with some tasty dirt on a bigger fish. I'm relatively sure that in their mind, as they are re-asked the very same questions with the prospect of immunity on the table, then their thinking changes from "But I honestly don't know anything" to "Ok. What do they want me to say so that I can get the immunity deal?"

Ultimately, the investigators get what they want, or the individual goes to jail. In the case of Michael Cohen, probably in an attempt to make it *look* like his testimony was not coerced, he is still doing some jail time. But does anyone really believe that some kind of deal wasn't struck in exchange for damning testimony against Donald Trump when Cohen's initial jail time estimate was around 65 years, and then once he made his vague statement about the non-disclosure payments, his jail time was suddenly reduced to around 5 years?

Michael Cohen most likely asked himself, what do they want me to say? The investigators most likely gave a few leading hints on what they would like his testimony to be, and voila! A statement that is a complete reversal of previous statements. And oh, by the way, his family and their finances are suddenly ok as well.

I suppose these tactics are ok when criminal kingpins are being investigated, but I'm not so sure when it comes to regular citizens. When the investigators squeeze a mafia hit man to get at the big boss, that might be ok, especially when murder is involved, but when they use the same tactics on regular citizens, it suddenly becomes a little frightening at the power that the investigators wield.

If these poor individuals, who were caught up in this solely for the reason of being close to Donald Trump had nothing to offer, then they would not get immunity. The investigators are not going to give anyone immunity unless they have something to offer in return. There is one caveat to this that is discussed in the chapter "Equal Justice Under the Law...Not".

So, if the Russian interference was proven, and there is no evidence of collusion, then why are the investigators still investigating? Moreover, what are they investigating?

The answer is obvious, everyone knows it, Republicans and Democrats alike, but the Democrats pretend that they are unaware. The obvious answer is that the investigators are not investigating the crime of election interference, they are following unrelated threads of evidence, trying as hard as they can to find something, anything that could be construed as a crime against Donald Trump.

First it was Russian interference. That could not be proven against the Trump campaign. Russian nationals were involved, but the Justice Department made it clear that there were no Americans who were knowingly involved.

Then it was Russian collusion. Which, interestingly, wouldn't be a crime even if it did occur since collusion is not a crime. Nevertheless, there is no evidence of the Trump campaign colluding with the Russians.

On to Obstruction of Justice. After all, President Trump fired James Comey. Since Comey was part of the investigative team on Russia, then the liberals would have you believe that Trump should not be able to fire him, because he would then be obstructing justice. Except, that everyone including Democrats and Republicans believe that Comey was doing a terrible job and should not have been in the position as head of the FBI.

It is now known, through Comey's own testimony, that he made insubordinate decisions by not consulting with his boss, and that he leaked information to the public as a means to affect the political process. Both of which are fireable offenses.

To make matters worse for the hope of Obstruction of Justice, President Trump fired Comey based partly on a recommendation from the Deputy Attorney General, Rod Rosenstein, who is the acting Director of the FBI on all things Russian, because Attorney General Jeff Sessions recused himself from the Russian investigation.

Rosenstein outlined the reasoning for Comey to be fired and President Trump acted on it. The liberals point to Trump stating that he was already thinking about firing Comey before Rosenstein's letter was even drafted. Therefore, Obstruction of Justice!

This is typical Trump Derangement Syndrome lunacy. President Trump was already thinking of firing Comey. Are you kidding? Of course, he was. Comey made a laughing stock of the FBI with the circus antics of his reports to the media about the Hillary Clinton investigation. Before he was fired, the liberals were decrying Comey's actions, blaming him for the Clinton loss, and demanding that he be fired. When he was finally fired, they forgot about what they said the day before and started yelling Obstruction of Justice!

The public sees through this however, and the Special Counsel investigators realize that there is no legal or constitutional leg to stand on here. So now we are back to collusion. After all, Trump's son, Donald Trump Jr. had a meeting with the Russians. Forget about the fact that it was one meeting. Forget that there was never any follow up and nothing happened afterwards. Somehow, just because he had a meeting, that is supposed to be collusion and illegal.

The absurdity of the left and the hypocrisy is palpable. Hillary Clinton's campaign paid for the Trump Dossier from Fusion GPS. Fusion GPS wrote the dossier based on input from Christopher Steele, a former intelligence officer of Britain's MI6 Intelligence Service.

Christopher Steele was then paid for this false information which he received from unknown "Russian sources".

In a nutshell, the Clinton Campaign paid for phony Russian opposition research about Trump that was then used by the FBI to spy on the Trump Campaign.

Have you heard the outcries from the left about how this information was gathered, and that the Hillary Clinton Campaign helped to fund the dossier? Have you heard the outcries on the left of how Steele gathered his information from the Russians? No, you have not heard any outcries. It is not expedient for the liberals to apply the same rules to the dossier as they do to the Trump Jr meeting. It is much more beneficial to pretend that the dossier did not happen, and then crucify Trump Jr. for a simple, legal meeting that went nowhere.

When it benefits the left, they will embrace it and it becomes an incessant talking point. When it does not benefit the left, they become blind, deaf, and dumb.

The Snowflake Epidemic

When I was eleven years old, I remember playing outside all of the time. On school days, I would get home, do my homework, and then go outside with my friends until eight o'clock. On the weekends, I would be outside after breakfast and wouldn't return home until it became dark, only returning quickly during the day for bathroom visits and to wolf down lunch and dinner.

We would often walk about a mile to the local pond, deep in the woods, and go swimming. Or we would play hockey, constantly moving and replacing our hockey nets as cars would pass on the street. We would walk to the local store and get snacks and drinks. We would go into the woods and play army, or hide and seek. We did all of this with no adult supervision.

Children today, on the other hand, are rarely seen outside. Take a drive through some of the neighborhoods in your town. It looks like a scene from an old horror movie, where you are the last person on earth. There are literally no children playing in the streets anymore. There are a lot of houses, and a lot of children. But they are all tucked safely inside their homes. Playing video games and watching television.

What happened? Why have things changed so much when it comes to children?

There is no single clear answer, but there are many possibilities.

One contributor is instantaneous news. When I was a kid, the news was on at six o'clock in the morning, twelve noon, six o'clock in the afternoon, and eleven o'clock at night. It was on for a half hour or an hour at a time. Since the available time slots were so limited, the news reports had to be very focused, usually on local stories.

So, for me living in Massachusetts, if something happened in Boston, I heard about it. If something happened in Maine, I didn't. If a child was abducted in Massachusetts, we all locked our doors at night. If a child was abducted in Pennsylvania, we were none the wiser.

That is not the case today. When a child is abducted anywhere in the United States, I'll know about in hours. There are now twenty-four hour news stations. These news stations need fresh news to report every single day. When something happens anywhere in the United States, we are now instantly aware.

What this does, is cause a false sense of insecurity. Forty years ago, if something happened a few towns away, we wouldn't even know. Now if something happens anywhere in the United States, it is reported on every news outlet instantaneously.

This makes it appear that there is something bad happening all of the time. This is true in a sense, but it is like lightning. Lightning is always striking somewhere in the world, but we don't really need to worry about it unless it's in our own neighborhood.

This false sense of insecurity makes us want to shelter our kids from the evils that lurk outside our homes. The result is children who have never experienced being alone without adults. Children who are never charged with the responsibility of looking out for themselves.

We shelter our children and never let them go anywhere alone. But does it really prevent? What we are fearful of in the first place? Has anyone heard of a child being abducted recently? The answer is unfortunately, yes. There are bad people in the world, and if they want to do harm, they will. All we can do is teach our children how to stay aware and how to react in these types of situations.

By not giving them responsibility and freedom, we inadvertently do not prepare them for the real world. When they become adults, they begin their careers believing that the world is responsible for their wellbeing because they have never learned to be responsible for themselves.

Respect is another thing that is clearly lacking in youth today. Many children respect no one, and they are being taught to respect no one.

It is evident everywhere. When I go out for dinner, there are parents with young children. The children are loud, rude, and totally oblivious to the people around them. They show no concern or consideration and are only interested in themselves and what they perceive as fun.

The parents display an aura of entitlement. They are out having dinner. They are paying for their meal. So, in their mind, that gives them license to do whatever they want. I am not one to call these people out. I am more likely to eat quickly and leave. But I have seen others call these parents out. The usual response is something like "If you don't like it, don't look!" or "I'm paying for my meal, the same as you!"

The one common factor is that these parents do not have any consideration for others. They then distill these values into their children. Ironically, these children are taught so well to be inconsiderate and to show no respect, that these behaviors are manifested back onto the parents themselves.

Occasionally, a parent will actually become embarrassed or ashamed of their child's behavior and attempt to reprimand the child to make them behave civilly. The child's classic response is to ignore the demands. The child obviously has no fear of punishment, and shows no signs of embarrassment or shame.

Eventually, the parent gives up, no longer feeling humiliated, content with the fact that they gave it a try.

Another large contributor to the snowflake epidemic is public schools and colleges. It is in these institutions where our children learn that everyone is equal, regardless of gender, regardless of athletic ability, and regardless of academic ability. It is a concept that is completely antithetical to reality.

Let's begin with gender. I hate to be the bearer of bad news, but there are only two genders. There is a male gender and a female gender. There are no more. Try as you might to redefine and create new genders, there are still only two. If you strip down any group of people, regardless of color, race, religion, political affiliation, or any other identifier, their genders are easily identifiable, and there are only two.

Changing a pronoun does not change the gender. A man who identifies as a woman is not a woman. A woman who identifies as a man is not a man.

The liberals in our society are actively trying to change how we think about these issues. Tolerance should always be practiced, but the left takes it one step further and celebrates these things, thereby normalizing them. Children are then exposed to ideas that they are too young to really be able to process. The result is liberal indoctrination of their young and susceptible minds.

Our poor children are subjected to a plethora of confusing ideals. They are being taught that they can change their gender when it suits them; that boys and girls have no differences; that using gender pronouns is discriminatory. They carry these ridiculous ideals into adulthood and become spoiled, self-entitled brats that have no preparation for life in the real world.

Children used to leave the home after high school or college and get their own place. Now, they stay with their parents through their twenties and thirties, because they were never prepared for life on their own.

Athletic ability has also been redefined by the left. When I was a kid, the boys on the football team were the biggest, strongest, most athletically fit boys in the school. The girls cheerleading team was filled with the most physically fit and talented girls in the school.

But the liberals have changed all of that. Sports are no longer dominated by the best of the best. In the liberal age of equality, you must allow kids who are not qualified onto these teams. If the coach or the school do not follow these unwritten rules, then they will be branded as intolerant bullies.

It may feel good in the moment to coddle the kids who do not have athletic ability, and to watch them with false pride on the field as they lose the game for their team, but it does not teach them about real life. When they finally begin their career in the real world, there are no businesses that are going to hire them because they are less qualified, there are no bosses who are going to watch with pride as they lose a major account.

The best thing this child could ever learn, is that they did not qualify to be on the team. If they truly want to be on the team, then they will have to get in better shape, practice and try out again the following year.

Academic ability is the same sad state. I don't blame the teachers, I blame the system. There are a few far left teachers who definitely hold views that are way outside the norm, but my interest is the mainstream public-school system. The teachers are forced to follow a specific curriculum, and teach to the ridiculous tests that have been devised by non-teacher, academic elites who have never taught a day in their lives.

The new normal is that all children are equal. If a child has difficulty taking tests, then that child must have a condition that causes stress during test taking. So that child is allowed to take the test alone, and for a longer period of time. If a child is having difficulty with a subject, they are diagnosed with ADD or ADHD, given a pill and pushed to the next grade.

What ultimately happens is that the student eventually graduates high school, never having to face adversity. Everything that child had difficulty with was swept under the rug. An alternate, easier route was always presented.

Once in college, our children are bombarded with liberal ideas. Everyone is exactly equal. Everyone deserves a good grade, regardless of effort or actual achievement. Nobody has the right to say something to you that makes you feel uncomfortable. If you do feel uncomfortable for any reason, then you can go to your safe space until those bad feelings have subsided.

If someone has a point of view that does not fit with your point of view, do you debate them like the old days? No, you can get a gang of friends together and shut them down. Squash their voice. Never allow their point of view to be heard. Kick them off campus.

This is the college of today. What was once a bias free zone for the discussion and debate of different ideas is now a one-sided, biased group of thugs that new students must conform to or be driven out.

These liberal students, who deny the right of free speech of others, decry fascism. Yet it is they who are demonstrably fascist.

Equal Justice Under the Law...Not

The Fourteenth Amendment states that we are all equal under the law. That means that all of the laws that apply to me also apply to politicians, entertainers, presidents, and you.

The punishments are also supposed to be equal. If I commit a crime and get five years in prison, then that same punishment should also apply to those members of society who are rich, powerful, and famous who have committed the same crime. There are some circumstances that might affect an outcome, such as previous convictions, history of abuse, and other factors. However, with all of these factors being equal, then the punishment should be the same regardless of wealth, power, or fame.

But is it true? Let's look at some comparisons.

Mishandling Classified Information
According to Politico on March 9, 2018.

Petty Officer First Class Kristian Saucier pleaded guilty in May 2016 to two felony counts, one for unlawful retention of national defense information and another for obstruction of justice, for taking cellphone pictures inside [a] Navy vessel and later destroying his own equipment upon learning he was under investigation.

Saucier took six pictures that were definitely classified. The Obama Justice Department sent him to jail for it.

At the same time, Hillary Clinton, during her tenure as Secretary of state decided to use her own private server, her own cell phones and her own private email account, rather than use the mandatory government secured servers and cell phones that are encrypted and secured by the US Government.

This was a conscious decision on her part to ensure that her emails would not be able to be seen by the US Government. When asked to provide the server for the investigation into her handling of classified information, she deleted over 30,000 emails, wiped the data from her computer using a data cleaning tool called Bleachbit, and physically had her cell phones destroyed.

From the FBI.GOV website, in his press conference on July 5, 2016, James Comey's initially states in his exoneration of Hillary Clinton, "From the group of more than 30,000 e-mails returned to the State Department, 110 e-mails in 52 e-mail chains have been determined by the owning agency to contain classified information at the time they were sent or received. Eight of those chains contained information that was Top Secret at the time they were sent; 36 chains contained Secret information; and eight contained Confidential information, which is the lowest level of classification."

Later in the same exoneration press conference, Comey states "Although there is evidence of potential violations of the statutes regarding the handling of classified information, our judgment is that no reasonable prosecutor would bring such a case."

So, Comey states that there *is* evidence of potential violations, lays out the evidence, and then states that no charges will be brought. Instead of doing his job and presenting his findings to the Attorney General, Loretta Lynch, Comey decides on his own that no "reasonable" prosecutor would ever bring the case.

Let's recap:

Case 1: A United States Navy Sailor takes six classified pictures of a nuclear submarine on his cell phone to brag about where he worked, then destroys his phone when realizing he was under investigation.

Verdict by the Obama Justice Department: Saucier was indicted and convicted in October 2016. He spent one year in prison and was still required to wear an ankle bracelet when pardoned by President Trump on March 9, 2018.

Case 2: A Former Secretary of State knowingly mishandles classified information by storing at least 110 classified emails on private, unsecure cell phones and a private, unsecure server that may have been compromised by foreign governments. Once realizing that she was under investigation, Hillary Clinton illegally deleted 30,000 emails and attempted to destroy the server as well as physically destroying her private, unsecure cell phones.

Verdict by the Obama Justice Department: No indictment.

The cases of Kristian Saucier and Hillary Clinton highlight the hypocrisy of the left. Both cases show very poor judgment, disregard for classified material, and obstruction of justice. However, the lesser crime being perpetrated by a sailor, and the larger crime being perpetrated by a Secretary of State, only further emphasize the favoritism that was shown Hillary Clinton by the Obama Justice Department.

Comey was demonstrably negligent in his duties. The liberals like to claim that Hillary Clinton was innocent because James Comey said so, but if you read through Comey's exoneration address, it is painfully evident that he had the evidence and chose not to pursue it because of his own biases. Liberals like to blame Comey as one of the reasons that Hillary Clinton lost the election, but had there been a truly unbiased Director of the FBI during the

Clinton email probe, then Hillary Clinton would probably have been indicted.

Immunity from Prosecution

When prosecutors and investigators have their sights set on someone to bring to justice, they have the power of the government behind them. They have unlimited resources, unlimited time, access to all of the databases, and the power to protect an individual from prosecution in exchange for their testimony against the real target of the investigation.

The way it usually works, is that the lesser criminals will have provable crimes by which the investigators could indict them. The investigators will dangle jail time, financial ruin, family ruin, and any other means available to cause the criminal to "flip". When a criminal flips, then they will spill all of the dirty details of the larger criminals unlawful deeds. If the details aren't tasty enough for the investigators, the lesser criminal could always embellish and add a few meatier, albeit non-existent details.

The danger of this, is that the investigators could potentially use false, fabricated evidence to get their conviction of the top guy. To a lot of investigators, this apparently doesn't matter.

Sometimes, the immunity can flow up. A really small criminal can be threatened with jail time or financial ruin so that he flips on a medium criminal. Then the medium criminal can be threatened with prison and financial ruin so that he will flip on the top guy. That was the case with Paul Manafort.

Rick Gates was threatened with prosecution and thus was given immunity by the Mueller team in exchange for his testimony against Manafort.

However, we all know that Manafort was not the target of Mueller. What Mueller was really attempting to do was to threaten Manafort with prison time and financial ruin so that he would then flip to provide evidence against Donald Trump.

The problem for Mueller, is that Manafort had nothing to give, and he was too proud to make something up. So the trial went forward and Manafort was convicted of Finance Fraud.

The liberals were ecstatic when Manafort was convicted. They say that this is a big win for the Mueller probe on the investigation into Donald Trump and Russian Collusion.

But wait a minute. What does Finance Fraud, which happened years before the Trump Campaign, have to do with Russian Collusion? That is the right question to ask. The answer of which, is nothing. It has nothing to do with it. Mueller was trying his best to dig up something.... anything on Manafort that would be felonious enough to warrant jail time. This could then be dangled in exchange for testimony.

But Manafort had nothing to give. Did he commit crimes? Evidently so, but his biggest crime, based on Mueller's actions, is that he worked for Donald Trump's campaign team for less than three months. Had Manafort never worked for Trump, he would never have been tried. That doesn't make it right or wrong, but it does underscore how ruinous the immunity from prosecution methods used by prosecutors can be.

The same happened to Michael Cohen, who was facing 65 years in prison. Suddenly he was only given 3-5 years after he completely changed his story and gave vague remarks for hush money payments by stating "at the direction of a candidate for federal office."

Both of these men, Gates and Cohen, were given immunity or less jail time in exchange for testimony, but what about the Hillary Clinton email investigation? The whole point of immunity is to get the person to flip and give information on the real target of the investigation.

In the wrong hands, however, immunity can work the other way. If the investigators are not honest, and they are sympathetic to the target of the investigation, then immunity can be used to prevent potential witnesses from testifying against the target.

With this in mind, let's look at the immunity deals surrounding the FBI investigation of the Clinton email probe.

Cheryl Mills –State Department Chief of Staff under Hillary Clinton – Given immunity from prosecution around September 23, 2016 in exchange for nothing.

John Bentel – Former director of the State Department's Office of Information Resources Management during Hillary Clinton's tenure as Secretary of State – Given immunity from prosecution around September 23, 2016 in exchange for nothing.

Heather Samuelson – Aide to Hillary Clinton – Given immunity from prosecution around September 23, 2016 in exchange for nothing.

Paul Combetta – The computer specialist who deleted Hillary Clinton's emails after ordered by Congress to preserve them – Given immunity around from prosecution around September 8, 2016 in exchange for nothing.

Bryan Pagliano – Technical Expert who set up Hillary Clinton's unsecured email server – Given immunity from prosecution in exchange for nothing.

The list above is basically everyone who would be directly involved with Hillary Clinton's email probe except Hillary Clinton herself. So, after everyone is given immunity without providing testimony or evidence against anyone, then who would be left to prosecute?

They all have deals so they cannot be prosecuted, but no information was given in return.

So, what was the immunity for? If it wasn't to ensnare the big fish, in this case Hillary Clinton, then it must have been to protect her. Rick Gates was given immunity, but he at least gave damaging testimony about Manafort, true or not.

After looking at how Paul Manafort, Rick Gates, and Michael Cohen were treated, and contrast that to the Clinton Probe immunities, then it becomes abundantly clear that the immunities given in the Clinton Probe were not to get information. The immunity from prosecution was given to *prevent* them from giving information.

If only Manafort and Cohen had committed their financial crimes in conjunction with a Democrat and steered clear of the Trump Campaign, then they would most likely be sipping Pina Coladas on a beach somewhere, enjoying their retirement.

In December of 2017, General Michael Flynn, who was the former National Security Advisor for President Trump, entered a guilty plea for lying to the FBI. Interestingly, the FBI agents who interviewed him said that they did not believe that General Flynn lied, but Mueller decided that he did. Flynn was not given immunity and never claimed to have anything disparaging to say about President Trump. The Fake News media will report that Flynn was offered a plea deal if he cooperated with Mueller on the Russia investigation. This is an insinuation that Flynn has information on Donald Trump or the Trump Campaign that could be used against President Trump.

However, a logical look at this shows how absurd the media narrative is. If Flynn flipped to give information about Trump, then he would have been given immunity. Also, the idea of cooperating as having some alternate meaning of something more than just simple cooperation with the investigators is again absurd. Flynn cooperated all along. He has nothing to hide and nothing to give. He never had a reason not to cooperate.

In October of 2017, George Papadopoulos pled guilty of lying to the FBI. In the Statement of the Offense in The Unites States of America vs George Papadopoulos, Mueller's team lays out all of the statements and communications from Papadopoulos that prove that he did in fact lie, although many of the "lies" are quite laughable. In the world of Special Persecutors and FBI Investigators, a lie, is a lie, is a lie.

For example, if you are being interviewed by an investigator, and you describe a man as being overweight, but in fact the man is very thin, then you have just lied to investigators and you now face prison time. Once you see the man, you might realize that you confused him with someone else, but that doesn't matter to the investigators. A far as they are concerned, you lied.

If your best recollection was that you met someone before an event occurred, but then it can be proven by investigators that you actually met them after the event occurred, then you just lied to investigators and now face prison time.

This is why the perjury trap is such a real problem when cases like these are being tried. Almost every threatened indictment is due to lying.

If you are the one being investigated, think of what you're up against in the interview with the investigators. They have hundreds of people, working full time, day after day, drudging up every available document related to you. Every email, text, phone record, correspondence, work record, and every other document that exists that can be used against you. To make matters worse for you, they have the unlimited power, unlimited time, and unlimited funds of the government.

When the investigators begin interrogating you, the start asking questions about timeline. When did this happen, relative to that? You must search your memory and attempt to recall the actual timeline.

Imagine being asked, did you meet a specific individual before or after your child's fifth birthday? Being a good citizen, you attempt an answer, not realizing the full extent of the law if your answer is wrong. So you say you are sure it was before. Then the interrogator throws down the text message from three years ago that proves that you actually met the person just after your child's fifth birthday.

Bad news for you. You just lied to the investigators and are now facing prison time.

This is a ridiculous example, but it highlights the absurdity of how the investigators can turn your own statements against you. After reading the Statement of the Offense for Papadopoulos, what I realized is that if I were ever brought in for an "interview" by an investigative agency, I would say that I don't recall to every question related to a timeline.

Do I believe that Papadopoulos misled the Mueller investigators? Yes, I do. Does it rise to the level of Prison time? I'm not sure.

I have trouble reconciling this tactic that is used by the FBI and other agencies when no crime was committed. If Papadopoulos actually committed a crime, I would be more receptive to the perjury accusations.

But the truth is, that the only charges that the Mueller team brought against Papadopoulos is lying and omissions. Lying and omissions about communications with Russian Nationals that are not against the law. Lying and omissions about an attempt to make a meeting occur between Trump and Putin, which is not against the law. The meeting never occurred between Trump and Putin, and the meeting never occurred with individuals beneath Trump and Putin. The meeting never occurred.

Papadopoulos was scared. He was interrogated with the full knowledge that he communicated with a Russian Professor and a female Russian National, and that the Mueller team was actively trying to find evidence that would tie Donald Trump with Russian Collusion.

Papadopoulos knew he was in trouble. Not because he did anything wrong, but because he knew that he was being interrogated by someone who already determined that Trump was guilty, and whose job was to now find the evidence to fit the crime.

Papadopoulos was a pawn and he knew it. As it is in the game of chess, pawns are sacrificed to capture the more powerful pieces. Now Papadopoulos would be sacrificed in an attempt to capture Donald Trump.

What Papadopoulos did while communicating with the Russian Professor was perfectly legal. Mueller has no charges against Papadopoulos other than lies and omissions.

But if you listen to the media, they make it sound as if Mueller had something more on Papadopoulos. They make it sound as if something sinister was happening with his communications with the Russian Nationals.

Did the Russians have something more sinister in mind? Absolutely! That's what they do. They are not our friends.

But just communicating with them does not make collusion. Meeting with them does not make collusion.

Trying to create a working relationship with them does not make collusion.

I think the most interesting "evidence" that the Mueller team offers in the Statement of the Offense document, is a communication dated August 15, 2016. This is directly from the Department of Justice website:

21. From mid-June through mid-August 2016, PAPADOPOULOS pursued an "off the record" meeting between one or more Campaign representatives and "members of president putin's office and the mfa."

a. For example,-on or about June 19, 2016, after several email and Skype exchanges with the Russian MFA Connection, defendant PAPADOPOULOS emailed the High Ranking Campaign Official, with the subject line "New message from Russia": "The Russian ministry of foreign affairs messaged and said that if Mr. Trump is unable to make it to Russia, if a campaign rep (me or someone else) can make it for meetings? I am willing to make the trip off the record if it's in the interest of Mr. Trump and the campaign to meet specific people."

b. After several weeks of further communications regarding a potential "off the record" meeting with Russian officials, on or about August 15, 2016, the Campaign Supervisor told defendant PAPADOPOULOS that "I would encourage you" and another foreign policy

advisor to the Campaign to "make the trip{], if it is
feasible."

c. The trip proposed by defendant PAPADOPOULOS
did not take place.

What the Mueller team ultimately has from
Papadopoulos is communications from Papadopoulos
indicating that, as of August 15, 2016, no meeting ever
occurred between Trump and Putin, and no meeting ever
occurred with Papadopoulos and anyone from the Russian
Government.

This is about two and a half months before the
general election. If the supposed collusion did not occur
by September of 2016, only two months before the
elections, then how could it have occurred at all?

Let's recap:

Case 1: People who are associated with the Russian
Interference investigation of the Trump Campaign are
spied on, have assets seized, and are indicted for
unrelated crimes or lying to investigators.

Case 2: People who are associated with the Clinton
Email Investigation are given immunity from prosecution.
None are indicted, and none offer anything in return for
their immunity.

A Spy in Our Midst

About five years ago around 2013, Dianne Feinstein was told by the FBI that her driver, who was working for her since 1996, was a Chinese Spy. The FBI correctly notified her so that the crime in progress could end. She immediately fired the man and most likely went into damage control mode to figure out what might have been compromised to the Chinese Government.

When it came to the Donald Trump Campaign, there was reason to believe that the Russians were attempting to infiltrate and meddle in the United States general election of 2016. According to PJ Media:

The threat assessment stage of the FBI's investigation in 2016 likely occurred sometime in late winter/early spring because former Attorney General Loretta Lynch testified that she met with Comey about the intelligence "matter" during this period. At this early stage, she and Comey decided not to tell the Trump campaign about possible national security threats regarding his campaign. When the topic was revisited in late spring, they again decided to say nothing.

But why would the Attorney General, Loretta Lynch, and the Director of the FBI, James Comey, decide not to inform an American politician that the Russians might be trying to meddle in the elections? Especially a politician who was running for president at the time.

Moreover, the FBI inserted a spy into the Trump campaign. The liberals call him an informant, as if there's a distinction, but the fact is, someone was placed in the White House to get information for the FBI. Why would the FBI plant a spy into the Trump campaign if not for an attempt to extract damaging evidence against Donald Trump?

Why did the FBI *choose* to notify Diane Feinstein about a spy plot and *choose* not to notify Donald Trump?

I wish I could think of an impartial, fair-minded reason, but the only reason that could possibly be true, is that it was political. The Obama Justice Department was obviously biased in favor of the Hillary Clinton Campaign and *wanted* the Russians to infiltrate the Trump Campaign, with the hopes that something illegal would occur so that the Justice Department could then bring charges against Donald Trump or his campaign. The result of which would be Clinton taking the presidency.

Unfortunately for the Democrats and for Hillary Clinton, Donald Trump did nothing wrong, his campaign did nothing wrong, and Clinton lost the election.

Let's recap:

Case 1: A Chinese Spy is discovered in the employ of Dianne Feinstein by the FBI. The FBI promptly notifies her and the spy is removed.

Case 2: The FBI discovered evidence of Russian Interference during the 2016 presidential campaign. Instead of notifying the Trump Campaign in the interests of national security, the FBI instead inserts their own spy into the Trump Campaign and let's everything play out.

Campaign Finance

Politico reported on January 4, 2013, that the Obama 2008 Campaign was fined $375,000 for breaking campaign finance laws. Politico states:

The major sticking point for the FEC appeared to be a series of missing 48-hour notices for nearly 1,300 contributions totaling more than $1.8 million — an issue that lawyers familiar with the commission's work say the FEC takes seriously. The notices must be filed on contributions of $1,000 or more that are received within the 20-day window of Election Day.

These violations resulted in a fine of $375,000 that was paid by the Obama Campaign and the Democratic National Committee. This was the extent of the punishment.

In the case of Donald Trump's Campaign, two women claiming to have had affairs with Trump years before signed non-disclosure agreements in exchange for money, which is entirely legal. Companies do it all the time.

Liberals claimed that it was a campaign violation by assuming, and hoping, that it was paid for by the Trump Campaign. However, it was proven to be from Donald Trump's personal finances and not the campaign.

But let's play Devil's Advocate for a moment and pretend that it was from the Campaign. Then what?

According to the Democrats, it is grounds for impeachment. It is proof that he must be removed from office immediately because he broke the campaign finance laws. But if it were even true, the only law the campaign would be charged with is failure to report the donations.

Fortunately, the Democrats do not have control of Congress. If they do get control in the 2018 elections, then President Trump's agenda will shut down and the economy, which is better than it has been in decades, will begin to slow down. The Democrats will attempt to impeach the President and the country will return to the fledgling Obama era politics.

Let's recap:

Case 1: Trump legally uses his own personal finances, on the order of $130,000 and $150,000, to seal two separate and legal non-disclosure agreements. The Democrats, if given the chance, would use this as grounds for impeachment.

Case 2: Obama violates campaign finance laws by not reporting $1,800,000 in donations. He is fined $375,000.

All of these true events emphasize the stark difference in how the Obama era Democrats were treated compared with Trump era Republicans. To say that the Republicans are being treated unfairly is an understatement.

Democrats - Immunity	Republicans – Indictments
Democrats - Exoneration	Republicans – Prison
Democrats - Fines	Republicans - Impeachment

When it comes to Democrats, Lady Justice has evidently removed her blindfold. It is no wonder that President Trump is so critical of The Justice Department. People like myself are just shaking our heads in disbelief over the events of the last few years.

If one looks at the previous examples objectively, one can only wonder if a more befitting agency name under the Obama Administration would have been the United States Department of Injustice.

ICE, the Police, and Other Heroes

When the police respond to a routine traffic stop or a domestic violence call, what is the first thing that happens? Out come the cell phones. Everyone in viewing distance is hoping that something will happen so that they can upload their video to YouTube and hope it goes viral.

Then an interesting thing happens. The perpetrators, whether white, black, or Hispanic, realize they are being recorded, and suddenly become emboldened. Their fear of being arrested is replaced by a desire to "stand up" to the police and taunt them. To try and make the police react so that they can be on YouTube, or perhaps so that they can try and win a big fat lawsuit from the state for police brutality.

The taunting escalates and as the video progresses, one wonders how the police can maintain their cool amidst so much hatred. Several people in the crowd also begin provoking the police, and thankfully, almost all of the time, the police remain imperturbable.

This is also a technique of the fascist group, Antifa. If you watch videos of Antifa "protests", you will see a group of people who are embracing anarchy. They use thug tactics like destroying property and setting cars on fire, all the while chanting that they are against fascism. They wear masks and brandish weapons. The main goal being to stop any and all political points of view that they disagree with. In other words, although Antifa stands for anti-fascism, they are fascists.

A favorite tactic of Antifa is to get in the face of the police who are trying to maintain the peace during Antifa protests. The Antifa supporters will push the police, throw rocks and other objects at the police, and spew a litany of profanities at the police, all in the hopes that the police will respond in kind. They perpetrate brutality on the police, all in the hopes of a response so that they can get a video highlighting "police brutality" for the fake news feed.

They want the police to engage them. They want to be able to display their protest on cable news and show how the police brutalized them. The liberal news organizations will accommodate. If the police do respond to the hate group by arresting the violent protesters, then what you will see on the liberal news shows is "professional" analysis on how the police are acting like a police state and brutalizing defenseless, peaceful demonstrators.

This of course, is nowhere near the truth. The provocation by the hoodlum protesters will never be discussed. The only thing of concern is the police reaction.

This is how liberal news drives a narrative, rather than actually reporting the news. They will leave out details that go against their narrative. They often creatively edit so that their narrative of police brutality can be portrayed as truth, all the while knowing that it is completely false.

When I was a child, I had a healthy respect for the police. I didn't fear them, but I did fear being arrested. If I saw a police officer, I would always say hello. They were always cordial and respectful to me as well.

What happened? Why are the police suddenly being portrayed as bad?

Throughout my life, I have had many friends and acquaintances. As jobs changed and my home base changed, these people come and go. Occasionally, I have known parents that use the police as a method of discipline. They would say, "Stop doing that or I'll call the police and they'll come and arrest you", or "If you don't listen to me, the police will take you away."

I have always believed that his method of discipline is flawed. The parents do this because they don't want to be seen as the bad guy to their children. They want to be friends with their children, not parents. So they use the police as a disciplinary tactic. That way the parents can remain the good friend to the child and the police become the bad guy to fear.

It never works, because the threat can never be followed through. The child quickly realizes that it is an empty threat that is never followed through. The parent never gets control of the child, and the child is taught to fear the police. The child is taught that the police can come and take them away for any reason.

I myself have seen children become fearful and not want to approach a police officer at a carnival or some other event. These are children that I knew who were attending the event with me and my children. My children would gleefully go to the police officer and say hi, and then we would take a picture with my children and the police officer. The other parent's child was afraid to go near the police officer, lest they will be taken away. How sad that there are children like this who are actually taught to fear the police.

Parents aren't the only problem. Unfortunately, our previous President, Barrack Obama also helped to perpetuate this fear. Even worse, I believe that he set race relations back fifty years.

Race is a touchy, difficult subject to speak about. It is hard to say what is on your mind or you will be labeled a racist. What you say may not be racist, but just because it's *about* race, many equate that with being racist.

I am a white male, but let me give you my perspective on race.

I remember the 2007 Super Bowl very well. It was a great game. The Colts eventually defeated the Bears in a very exciting contest. The coaching, like most championship games, was skillful and extremely well done.

Around the second or third quarter, one of the announcers stated that this was an historic game, because both coaches were black. It was only then that it hit me. Tony Dungy and Lovie Smith were black. Up until that point, all I saw were two great coaches going head to head. I never once thought of them as black coaches. They were just coaches to me. Who cares what color their skin is? They were in the Super Bowl because of their great coaching. The only thing that I saw, was their coaching, and frankly, I believe that the announcer unwittingly took a little of their greatness away by making it about race instead of just leaving it about their skill and intelligence.

When the announcer made that statement, it made me realize how racism is continuously propagated. It is true that these two men are black. But why can't we look at them for their accomplishments rather than their color?

It's only when we try and say that that their accomplishment is amazing, *considering* their color, that we again make it about race rather than their abilities.

I know the announcer meant well, but I personally don't believe making statements like this helps race relations at all. We have to get past making the accomplishments about Whites, African Americans, Hispanics, Native Americans, Asians, or about race at all, and make the accomplishments about ability, intelligence, and character.

Another incident related to race happened to me during a family cookout. My brother-in-law at the time was invited to my house for a large family cookout. He asked if he could bring a friend and I said sure, no problem. I often had people who I did not know show up at family cookouts who were brought by the people that I had invited.

When they arrived, my brother-in-law introduced me to his friends. A lovely couple, who happened to be a black man and a white woman. They were pleasant, cordial, and a delight to speak with. I spent most of my time with the man, talking about kids, jobs, and other introductory types of conversations when you meet someone for the first time. Other than a hello, I did not really speak with his wife.

Interestingly, she resembled my brother-in-law's sister-in-law. A weird thing, but nevertheless true. When they left, we said our goodbyes and I didn't think much more of it.

About a year later, I was getting my eyeglasses repaired at a local eyeglass store. The woman behind the counter knew me immediately, because at the time I had very long blond hair, but I was having some trouble placing her. Then I realized that it was my brother-in-law's sister-in-law.

At least I thought it was her. I wasn't quite sure, but she was sure of who I was, and I didn't want to embarrass myself by not recognizing her, so I just acted like I knew her.

As she was repairing my eyeglasses, her husband walked in. It was the African American man from the cookout. I immediately recognized him because I spent half the cookout talking with him. I also immediately realized that the person working on my glasses was not who I thought it was, but was actually his wife.

I quickly rushed over to say hi. As I walked towards him I told him hi, and then told him how I didn't recognize his wife at first. At that time his wife appeared with my glasses.

He looked at me sternly and said, "Yeah, now that the black man shows up, you recognize us."

My eyebrows raised and my jaw gaped open. I was speechless.

Then he said, "I notice we never got an invite back to your house."

I was dumbfounded. I have met dozens of people that have come to my house, through others, as guests for a one-time visit. I don't ever remember following up on these one-timers. I am not saying I didn't enjoy their company, I almost always did, but I don't keep a list of all of the people I have ever met one time so that I can invite them to upcoming family functions. It's not an excuse, it's just a fact.

I usually have no problem speaking with people. But on this occasion, I just couldn't think of anything to say. The silence at that point was deafening. I grabbed my glasses, said goodbye, and quickly walked out of the store.

My point of this story, is that race never played into my thought process. The way I bumped into him, and the way that I discovered that his wife worked there, normally would have led to a friendly conversation. Instead, it destroyed the foundation that was already laid. He chose to make it about race, and ultimately that ruined our chance to have a great relationship.

Once I was able to come to my senses and I thought about it a bit. He believed that I was racist for not inviting him back to my home, but what he didn't even consider was that I at least invited him to my home once. He never invited me to his home at all. For some reason, he decided that my lack of action was racism, but his lack of action was ok.

I only mention these stories because it highlights one of the problems of race relations today. Most of the racism is manufactured. It doesn't really exist, but instead of looking at other, more realistic possibilities for people's actions, racism is offered as the only possibility.

This drives a narrative for liberals, a means to create division to further divide the political parties. The bottom line is, by driving a false narrative of racism, the liberals can boost their voting bloc by pushing a completely false narrative that Republicans are racist and Democrats are pro minority. This could not be further from the truth.

When President Obama became president, I didn't expect much from him in the way of any conservative principles, and he didn't disappoint me in that respect. But I did believe that an African American President was going to be great for race relations in America. This turned out to be a huge disappointment for me.

It all started with the Harvard Professor, Henry Louis Gates Jr, who was arrested in 2009.

He was returning home from a long trip to China. When he arrived home, he had trouble getting in his front door. So, he tried forcing it open. To a neighbor, it looked like someone was trying to break into the home, so they called the police.

When the police arrived, each man's account differs. Apparently, Professor Gates was upset that he was even being looked at as a criminal by Police Sergeant James Crowley because it was his own home. I might have felt the same way.

Words were exchanged, the level of the conversation escalated, and the result was the Professor being arrested for Disorderly Conduct, which was later dropped.

One thing that everyone knows, or should know, is that when dealing with the police you don't become argumentative, and you don't resist. Some people look at this as the police being all powerful and that somehow the police should be kept in check by letting them know who the boss is. Letting them know who pays their salaries.

The problem with this thought process, is that once you are allowed to *not* give the police respect and compliance, then what is left is anarchy. If one person doesn't have to listen to a cop then no one does. If one person is allowed to disobey a cop's demands, then no one has to obey.

Compliance and respect have to be a given when dealing with the police. Most of the violent incidents occur because the suspect is not complying. Somehow, not complying with the police has become ok. Many times, this non-compliance escalates into a violent situation, which then results in the suspect being arrested. The chances are very high that they may not have been arrested had they complied in the first place.

What President Obama should have done was to side with the system. Allow an investigation to occur and then comment on the results. Instead, as reported by CNN, he specifically jumps to race by stating:

"I don't know, not having been there and seeing all the facts, what role race played.

But I think it's fair to say, number one, any of us would be pretty angry; Number two, that the Cambridge Police acted stupidly in arresting somebody when there was already proof that they were in their own home; and, number three, that there's a long history in this country of African-Americans and Latinos being stopped by law enforcement disproportionately."

This was a terrible statement to make. He begins his statement by saying that he knew nothing about the facts of the case, and then immediately jumped to a conclusion of racism. It turned what should have been a simple case of two men losing control and escalating a situation, into an encounter about race.

In the Michael Brown case, where Brown was killed by the police after a robbery, the Attorney General under President Obama, Eric Holder, visited the family of Michael Brown, but not the family of the cop. The obvious insinuation being that Brown was killed because of his race.

The officer was later cleared of any wrong doing, but it was too late, his life was ruined.

I am not foolish. I know that racism still exists, but let's focus on real racism and not waste our time manufacturing it. If there truly is racism, then we must attack it head on. If a cop uses deadly force for the wrong reason, including racism, then he should be punished as a criminal. The police have too much power and must be held to a higher standard than the rest of us.

However, if a cop is forced to use deadly force because his or her life is truly in danger from a violent offender, then we must see it for what it is, cops protecting themselves and more importantly, protecting us.

When I hear of any incident where a cop is killed, it just makes me realize how difficult a police officer's job really is. Criminals don't like to get caught. Many will shoot police officers in an attempt to get away. Many times, those officers are killed.

Yet when some people are stopped by the police, all they think about is themselves. They feel singled out and want to confront the police. To yell at them. To act irrationally and escalate the situation.

What these people don't understand, or perhaps what they fully understand, is that when one person becomes agitated and escalates the situation with the police, then other people around them tend to begin escalating their actions as well. If the police don't quickly get control of a situation like this, then they will lose control and risk the chance of someone getting hurt, be it a cop, a bystander, or the offender.

Unfortunately, many times the quickest way to regain control of these situations is to arrest the first person who loses control. It is always easy to blame race, gender, or a host of other labels, but the truth almost always is because the person arrested became dangerously out of control and actually forced their own arrest.

Many of these situations are domestic violence where the offenders are not planning on committing crimes. Then there are those who commit violent crimes like rape, aggravated assault, and murder.

When it comes to violent crime, there are a lot of statistics that are thrown around. But statistics and percentages are a funny thing. They are numbers that can be manipulated to highlight a particular viewpoint. It may not be true, but numbers can be manipulated to make it *look* like it's true.

For example, a favorite statistic by the left, is that there is a disproportionate number of African American's who are shot by police when compared to White Americans. There are many news outlets who have the statistics to prove this.

For instance, The Washington Post reported:

"Black males accounted for 22 percent of all people shot and killed in 2017, yet they are 6 percent of the total population. White males accounted for 44 percent of all fatal police shootings, and Hispanic males accounted for 18 percent."

This is a true statistic, there is no doubt about it. However, the insinuation is that the disproportionality of the numbers is based on race. That African Americans are being singled out simply because of their race and that police are shooting them only because they are African American.

The "yet" that is in the Washington Post paragraph above is inserted purposely to highlight the apparent unexplainable disparity between white and black victims. Anyone with half a brain would see that the African American population was being singled out.

Before we come to this apparently obvious conclusion, let's take a look at another statistic. A statistic that is rarely given along with the Washington Post statistic above.

The US Department of Justice, through The Bureau of Justice Statistics, published a report that breaks down all violent crime committed from 2012 through 2015 by race of victim and race of offender. An interesting result can be seen. The offenders of all violent crime were 43.8% White, 22.7% Black, 14.4% Hispanic, and 2.2% other.

TABLE 1
Percent of violent victimizations, by race/Hispanic origin of victim and offender, 2012–2015

Race/Hispanic origin of victim	Average annual number	Race/Hispanic origin of offender							
		Total	White	Black	Hispanic	Other[a]	Single offenders of two or more races	Multiple offenders of various races[b]	Unknown race or number of offenders
Total violent victimizations[c]	5,833,800	100%	43.8%	22.7%	14.4%	2.2%	6.0%	2.8%	8.0%
White	3,679,410	100%	56.6*	14.7†	11.0†	1.7†	6.1†	2.1†	7.9†
Black	850,720	100%	10.9†	63.2*	6.6†	0.5!†	7.4†	4.0†	7.4†
Hispanic	846,520	100%	20.0†	20.5†	40.3*	2.5†	5.7†	3.3†	7.8†
Other[d]	198,320	100%	29.6†	18.9	9.7‡	17.5*	3.6!†	6.1!†	14.5
Persons of two or more races	258,830	100%	60.2*	13.8†	7.2†	2.3!†	3.9†	5.5†	7.1†

Note: Comparison groups are intraracial percentages (white-on-white, black-on-black, Hispanic-on-Hispanic, or other race-on-other race). White, black, and other race categories exclude persons of Hispanic or Latino origin. See appendix table 2 for standard errors.
*Comparison group.
†Significant difference from comparison group at the 95% confidence level.
‡Significant difference from comparison group at the 90% confidence level.
! Interpret with caution. Estimate based on 10 or fewer sample cases, or coefficient of variation is greater than 50%.
[a]Includes offenders perceived to be American Indian or Alaska Native or Asian, Native Hawaiian, or Other Pacific Islander.
[b]Mixed race group.
[c]Includes rape or sexual assault, robbery, aggravated assault, and simple assault.
[d]Includes victims who were American Indian or Alaska Native, or Asian, Native Hawaiian, or Other Pacific Islander.
Source: Bureau of Justice Statistics, National Crime Victimization Survey, 2012–2015.

Now if we align the statistic from The Department of Justice with the statistic from The Washington Post, we find that 22% of all people shot in 2017 were African American, and that 22.7% of all violent crimes from 2012 to 2015 were committed by African Americans.

By looking at only The Washington Post statistic, we can see that African Americans make up only 6% of the total population, *yet* 22% of the people shot by police were African American. Therefore, we can conclude that African Americans must be being singled out due to their race.

When we take into account The Department of Justice report, we can see that African Americans make up only 6% of the total population, *yet* they commit 22.7% of all violent crime. Now our conclusion is, since African Americans are committing a disproportionate amount of the violent crime, there is an equally disproportionate amount of police shootings. In fact, the percentage of the race of the violent offenders killed by police, aligns quite closely to the percentage of the race of the total violent offenders.

When looked at logically, it is clear that this another false narrative by the left to paint the police as racist. It is demonstrably untrue.

Unfortunately for American law enforcement, the liberals will never report the entire story. If they did, they would lose a vital link to their base. They need their base to remain ignorant of these facts so that they can keep a stark division between Republicans and Democrats. The liberals cannot let their constituents realize that they really do not have the best interests of their constituents in mind.

Chicago is a prime example of this. The usual liberal argument is that the strict gun laws in Illinois, and thus Chicago, would prevent gun violence if only they didn't have the less strict gun law states of Wisconsin and Indiana on their borders. The interesting premise of this argument is that if criminals who commit violent crimes could not get any guns at all from Wisconsin or Indiana, then gun violence would magically disappear from the Illinois statistics.

This is an extremely weak argument since the very premise assumes that violence is somehow related to the guns. If only the cities with the highest crime rates could only eliminate all guns, then overnight we would be in the ever-elusive liberal utopia.

In the real world, does anybody really believe that the problem is guns? Just following this argument to its logical conclusion means that the cities and counties across the United States that have the most guns *must* have the most violence. It makes perfect sense. Therefore, like Chicago, all of the liberal strongholds must have much less crime, due to the lack of guns, and all of the conservative strongholds must have much more crime, due to an overabundance of guns.

Let's approach this from a different angle. CBS News ranked the twenty-five most dangerous cities in the United States based on the violent crime occurrences per 100,000 residents. This list ranks the cities based only on violent crimes committed. A violent crime was defined by the FBI as murder, non-negligent manslaughter, rape, robbery, and aggravated assault.

Politico does a great job of identifying the 2016 general election results by county. So we can look at the political affiliations of the top twenty-five dangerous cities by the counties that these cities are in.

If we use this data, and then take a look at the political makeup of the city populations based on political affiliations, something interesting emerges.

	City	State	Violent Crime /100,000	Dem /Rep	County
1	Detroit	Michigan	2,047	Democrat	Wayne
2	St. Louis	Missouri	1,913	Democrat	St. Louis
3	Memphis	Tennessee	1,820	Democrat	Shelby
4	Baltimore	Maryland	1,780	Democrat	Baltimore
5	Rockford	Illinois	1,659	Republican	Winnebago
6	Kansas City	Missouri	1,655	Democrat	Jackson
7	Cleveland	Ohio	1,631	Democrat	Cuyahoga
8	Milwaukee	Wisconsin	1,533	Democrat	Milwaukee
9	Little Rock	Arkansas	1,531	Democrat	Pulaski
10	Oakland	California	1,421	Democrat	Alameda
11	Stockton	California	1,421	Democrat	San Joaquin
12	Indianapolis	Indiana	1,374	Democrat	Marion
13	Springfield	Missouri	1,337	Democrat	Greene
14	San Bernardino	California	1,324	Democrat	San Bernardino
15	Toledo	Ohio	1,192	Democrat	Lucas
16	Lansing	Michigan	1,164	Democrat	Ingham
17	Anchorage	Alaska	1,144	Republican	Anchorage
18	Washington	District of Columbia	1,132	Democrat	
19	Springfield	Illinois	1,116	Republican	Sangamon
20	Beaumont	Texas	1,112	Republican	Jefferson
21	Albuquerque	New Mexico	1,112	Democrat	Bernalillo
22	Buffalo	New York	1,110	Democrat	Erie
23	Minneapolis	Minnesota	1,109	Democrat	Hennepin
24	Chicago	Illinois	1,106	Democrat	Cook
25	Nashville	Tennessee	1,102	Democrat	Davidson

What immediately stands out, is that of the twenty-five cities with the worst violent crime, twenty-one of the twenty-five are controlled by liberals.

Could it be that the violence is not as simple as the availability of guns, but the policies of the liberal leaders? The table above clearly illustrates that there is a direct correlation between violent crime and the policies of the leaders. Nancy Pelosi and Chuck Schumer live in beautiful houses, make lots of money, and have no worries about crime in their neighborhoods. They are the leaders of the Democratic Party that oversee and manage most of the crime ridden cities and counties.

Yet year after year, nothing changes for the better. The cities and counties remain the same, or more often get even worse.

The Democrats then place the blame on the Republicans, who do not have direct control of these cities and towns. They place blame on guns and Supreme Court Justice picks, which have nothing to do with the day-to-day lives of their constituency. Rather than use the available money to bolster the neighborhoods that really need it, the money gets funneled to the elite neighborhoods that don't need it.

Don't believe that? Take a look around the areas of any liberal city or town. Look at the dilapidated, run down sections of town. How far back in time do you have to go before you can remember that city or town ever looking decent? For most of us, it is usually decades.

But why don't these areas ever get a makeover? Why do they perpetually remain run down?

There really is no reason other than the leaders choose to leave them that way. The people that live there become used to it. It becomes normal. When a local talks about that section of town, it's always with the unwritten knowledge that that is a bad area of town. An area to be avoided. Except, it's not totally avoided, because people are actually living there. They live their entire lives there and they think that this is how life is supposed to be.

Meanwhile, the liberals allow them to believe that, then do nothing to change the situation. The liberal leaders reap the rewards that the power of government gives them, and deny it to their constituents. The constituency is left unaware and is spoon fed lies and misdirection to keep them thinking that it is the "other guys" who are to blame. They are led to believe that it is the one percenters who are soaking up all of the available income so that the poorest Americans have none, seemingly oblivious that their leaders are the one percenters.

This is the message of the left. Blame the workers. Blame the doers. Create a generation of children who only know that society owes them a living. Society owes them a house, a car, a job, and a seventy-inch flat screen television.

Rather than give them help to find and hone their own abilities so that they can proudly make their own way through life, the liberals keep them underfoot, denying them the pride to take care of their own family. Showing them that their only recourse in life is to take from those that have earned it.

Finally, it is this self-centered, entitlement attitude that creates the crime. Without opportunities and with the learned liberal attitude of entitlement, the young generation turns to crime and social unrest. Working for a living is not an option since they honestly believe that they are now owed a living by the working class and by extension the rich. I wonder how many of these young soldiers of economic redistribution would give away their riches if they suddenly won the lottery.

The liberal policies in these high-crime cities have created an atmosphere of hate, and with the help of President Obama's policies towards race, have created a general feeling among the younger liberals that all police are bad. That somehow, police are something to be loathed and cannot be trusted.

The stand down policies given to the police by the Police Chiefs of these cities have not helped the situation Through inaction, this has created a mob that now *expects* and now demands that the police will no longer take action during their riotous behaviors.

The recent mob actions by Antifa highlight this as they burn cars, destroy buildings and property, and throw things at the police. The entire time that these horrible crimes are being committed, the police do nothing.

These liberal policies have created an atmosphere of hate towards the police, especially among young and ignorant liberals. But without the police, there would only be anarchy.

Imagine a city with no police department. When a crime is committed, there is no one to call. When you are fearful for the lives of your children because someone is breaking into your home, there would be no one to respond to your calls for help.

I know that this would never occur. There will always be police. That is one of the things that defines a civilization. But that doesn't mean that we would want the police to be all powerful either. Other countries have their own methods for policing. Some perhaps a little better, some far worse.

China, for example, imposes the death penalty at a much higher rate than the United States. According to Business Insider, even white-collar crimes like embezzling, bribery, illegal fund raising, and fraud are levied with the death penalty as punishment.

A person not knowing the facts might marvel at China's ability to keep their crime rate in check, without ever knowing that around four thousand citizens are executed every year. This is a true police state, where the fear of death is very real. The fear of death for what we would consider minor infractions that would only require jail time.

In our system, when individuals are killed by police, there must always be unbiased investigations to maintain a fair system of justice. But the liberals must start telling the truth on things like police shootings. Spinning the results as an attempt to gain more votes has got to stop. This includes all law enforcement officials.

More recently, the leaders of the Democratic Party have focused their unfounded ire on the United States Immigration and Customs Enforcement division, more popularly known as ICE.

Before we discuss this very important law enforcement agency, let's take a look at what ICE does.

According to the ICE website, ICE does the following:

ICE executes its mission through the enforcement of more than 400 federal statutes, and focuses on smart immigration enforcement, preventing terrorism and combating the illegal movement of people and trade.

Many people believe that the only function of ICE is to separate families at the border who are attempting to enter the country illegally. This could not be further from the truth. In fact, ICE is a very busy agency indeed. Below is an excerpt from the ICE website. It is important for this discussion to know what ICE actually does other than border security.

ICE'S mission is to protect America from the cross-border crime and illegal immigration that threaten national security and public safety.

This mission is executed through the enforcement of more than 400 federal statutes and focuses on smart immigration enforcement, preventing terrorism and combating the illegal movement of people and goods.

Immigration Enforcement

Immigration enforcement is the largest single area of responsibility for ICE. While certain responsibilities and close cooperation with U.S. Customs and Border Protection, U.S. Citizenship and Immigration Services, and others require significant ICE assets near the border, the majority of immigration enforcement work for ICE takes place in the country's interior.

ICE special agents strive to help businesses secure a lawful workforce and enforce immigration laws against those who encourage and rely on unauthorized workers, sometimes taking advantage of their situation to offer low pay and inadequate conditions.

Multiple programs help ICE focus and improve on stated priorities to find and remove illegal aliens who are criminals, fugitives or recent arrivals. Immigration enforcement entails cracking down on those who produce fraudulent documents to enable unlawful activity. Additionally, several robust efforts seek to continue improving the safe and humane detention and removal of persons subject to those actions.

Investigating Illegal Movement of People and Goods

ICE special agents, officers and attorneys enforce provisions of approximately 400 federal statutes. This large and diverse body of laws is reflected in the wide array of offices, programs and projects that make up ICE. People are smuggled and trafficked, while children are sexually exploited at home and abroad.

Illegal trade, in a very general sense, predominately involve guns, money and drugs, but ICE's responsibilities extend much further into all kinds of illegal and counterfeit merchandise coming into the country. For instance, ICE's responsibilities include the repatriation of cultural treasures out of the country to original owners abroad, and combatting the trade of child pornography and much more.

Preventing Terrorism

Most ICE offices and programs have a role in preventing terrorism. Several are on the front lines of this effort, either identifying dangerous persons before they enter the U.S. or finding them as they violate immigration or customs laws. ICE also works to prevent the illegal export of U.S. technology that could be used or repurposed to do harm.

ICE plays a vital role in keeping our country safe. Not only do they find and deport people who have entered our country illegally that are fugitives, criminals, or recent arrivals, but they also search for human traffickers, track down criminals involved in illegal trade of guns, money and drugs, combat child pornography and much, much more.

Why is it then, that the only thing we hear about is the illegal immigrants at the border?

It is the narrative that works for the liberals to attempt to highlight what they consider an injustice. The idea that families are being separated at the border plays well on television.

One of the big stories of 2018 were a couple of pictures showing children in detention cages. As it turned out, one of the pictures was taken during the Obama administration, and the other was a hoax picture taken at a Dallas, Texas rally. It is much more helpful to the liberal narrative for the liberal media to show these detention centers and attach them to the Trump Administration.

However, MSNBC, as reported by The Daily Caller, visited one of these detention centers and discovered that the children were not in cages and they were being treated quite well. They were separated from the adults that they entered illegally with, but that is necessary.

Since ICE also deals with human trafficking, they are aware that some of these children are brought illegally into the country to be sold through human trafficking, or to be used as a method for the adults to bypass the immigration system and gain entry into the United States. So the children and adults must be separated until ICE can prove that these adults are indeed the parent or legal guardian of the children.

Liberal leaders have chosen to use this necessity of vetting the adults as a rallying cry for the left to abolish ICE for crimes against humanity. This twisted argument only shows the extent that the left will go to so that they can attempt to gain votes and to regain power in Congress. Hopefully, the majority of Americans will see through this political ploy and keep the Democrats and Socialists away from immigration policy

ICE is an absolute necessity. It does not need to be abolished or rebuilt from the ground up, as the liberal members of Congress espouse. Instead, if they don't like some of the laws that Congress enacted and ICE is enforcing, then those in Congress have the power to change them.

During President Obama's first two years of his presidency, the liberals had full control of the House of Representatives and the Senate. They could have done something about the illegal immigration laws if they believed that they are unfair.

However, they chose to do nothing. The same laws that were in place during the Obama Administration are the exact same laws that are now in place during the Trump Administration. The one and only difference is that the Obama Administration chose to not enforce the laws as written, and the Trump Administration chose to obey and enforce the laws of the United States as they are written.

We cannot look at these law enforcement personnel as law breakers. It is the illegal immigrants who have entered our country illegally under false pretenses who are the law breakers. ICE agents put their lives on the line every single day to help keep Americans safe and secure.

There are only two classes of people who would benefit from the dissolution of ICE.

First, the liberal Democrats would now have unfettered access to put forth their plan to turn illegals into votes, thereby guaranteeing an increase in their voting bloc.

Second, the illegals themselves would no longer have a law enforcement agency that would be able to remove them. These illegals, and all of the illegals that would follow in droves, would be free to continue taking American social security numbers, taking American jobs, and taking American welfare benefits.

Luckily, so far, the dissolution of ICE is only a liberal and socialist talking point. I don't believe that the liberals would ever be able to dissolve the ICE agency, but if they take over the House and Senate, they will probably try very hard to make it happen.

ICE, local police, state police, and all law enforcement agencies are vital in the society of the United States. We give law enforcement power, but then we must remain vigilant to ensure that this power always remains in check. There are bad cops, and methods to deal with them. Sometimes it takes more time than it should to weed out these bad cops, but overall, we have a good system for policing the police.

Now if we can only teach our children to once again respect, and not fear, the law enforcement personnel who protect the greatest country on earth, perhaps we can regain the civility that we once had.

Media Bias
(aka: Fake News)

Fifty years ago, there were unwritten rules in the media. Guidelines that defined how news was gathered, how news was delivered, and above all, only reporting the facts.

A reporter would investigate a story, interview the people involved, gather facts, and if something news worthy came to light, that news organization would not run the story until it was verified using a second source. In many cases, the story would not run unless there were three independent sources.

But as cable news took a 24 hour, 7 days a week format, things started to change. News reporting morphed into news analysis. The news stations couldn't just report the same news, all day long, over and over. There had to be something else to fill the time, so the news anchors took on the roles of arbiters and analysts. Bringing on guest speakers to offer their analysis.

The three big news organizations, ABC, CBS, and NBC, became more and more liberal. Their views started slanting to the left, and their reporting began favoring liberal views.

In 1996, FOX News arrived on the scene to fill the void of conservative customers who had no news outlet to turn to for their daily news. Eventually, FOX News would come to dominate the news industry.

Although FOX News slanted right, they always presented the liberal points of view from the left, and continue to do so to this day.

When President Obama was in office, the big three news outlets were more of an extension of the Democratic machine than actual news organizations. President Obama could do no wrong in the eyes of the liberal media. When the news was delivered by the big three, it was always skewed to make President Obama look good.

Mark Humphrys of markhumphrys.com offers a detailed analysis of media bias during the Obama years. In particular, here a few interesting facts about the media coverage leading up to the 2008 general election:

- Newspapers were biased in favor of Democrats, with 59% positive stories and 11% negative stories. For Republicans, 26% of the stories were positive, and 40% were negative.
- The television networks ABC, CBS, and NBC were biased in favor of Democrats, with 40% positive stories and 17% negative stories. For Republicans, 19% of the stories were positive, and 37% were negative.

- For Cable TV, CNN has a similar bias as the television networks.
- MSNBC was more neutral with 47% positive stories and 19% negative stories. For Republicans, 38% of the stories were positive, and 30% were negative.
- Fox News was biased in favor of Republicans with 32% positive stories and 21% negative stories. For Democrats, 24% of the stories were positive, and 37% were negative.
- Fox News leans conservative, but is clearly less biased than newspapers and network television.

The analysis above clearly shows that the mainstream media was knowingly pushing a pro Obama agenda. This was done when John McCain was President Obama's opponent.

We're talking about John McCain, who was one of the nicest politicians you could ever meet. It only gets worse for Donald Trump.

The Federalist published an article in February of 2017 that lists 16 Fake News stories in the Month of January 2017 alone. Here are a few:

Transgender Suicides

After Trump's victory in November of 2016, there were rumors that transgender teens were committing suicide because Trump was elected. Obviously, the implication being that they had so much fear of what President Trump would do the transgender community, that ending their lives now made more sense than enduring the alternative.

These rumored stories were never and have never been verified as being true, but Zach Stafford, writer for The Guardian, tweeted the rumors as fact.

His tweet was retweeted more than 13,000 times before he deleted it. He later tweeted an explanation of why his original tweet was deleted, which was shared 7 times.

Although he "corrected" the record, the damage was done. 13,000 retweets that reached tens of thousands, or perhaps, hundreds of thousands of people.

The explanation tweet was not shared. When these tweets have an agenda behind them, which was making Trump look bad, the people who are retweeting are not interested in the truth, their only interest is the potential damage of the lie.

Nancy Sinatra's Complains About the Inaugural Dance Song Choice

At President Trump's inaugural ball, it was announced that he and the first lady's inaugural dance would be to the song "My Way", by Frank Sinatra. CNN reported that Nancy Sinatra, the daughter of Frank Sinatra, was not happy about this song choice.

When it was discovered that Nancy Sinatra never said this, CNN later corrected the article without any explanation.

The White House Climate Change Purge

On the day of President Trump's inauguration, the Time's published an article by writer Coral Davenport claiming that the Trump administration had purged climate change references from the White House website. The headline was obviously meant to incite anger in people who are passionate about climate change.

The purge did not happen, but the article was shared nearly 50,000 times on Facebook.

The Missing MLK Jr. Bust

On January 20, 2017, Time reporter Zeke Miller claimed that the bust of Martin Luther King Jr. was removed from the White House. An immediate controversy ensued.

When it was determined that the bust was in fact still there, Miller issued a correction.

This shows how "reporters" today actually report. Miller didn't even bother asking the White House about the bust. He just assumed it was removed because he didn't see it when he looked around. Evidently, someone was standing in front of it when he looked.

But rather than get the story correct and factual, he jumped to a conclusion that fit into his own bias about President Trump.

The Travel Ban Death

On January 31, a Fox affiliate station out of Detroit reported that "A local business owner who flew to Iraq to bring his mother back home to the US for medical treatment said she was blocked from returning home under President Trump's ban on immigration and travel from seven predominately Muslim nations. He said that while she was waiting for approval to fly home, she died from an illness."

The original article was immediately shared 123,000 times and 9,000 times from other sources. "Reporters" quickly latched onto the story and shared the story thousands and thousands of times. The story took off because it fit precisely with the liberal notion of President Trump discriminating against Muslim's with impunity.

However, once the real reporters began investigating, they discovered that the man had lied about when his mother actually died. The entire story was a fabrication, and since the original "reporters" had not bothered to verify the account, the story made its way into the American public as a factual, well investigated story.

Once the truth came to light, the Fox affiliate quietly corrected the story, but once again, the damage was already done.

There are 16 of these fake news stories, propagated by the liberal media, in a blatant attempt to disparage the President of the United States. All 16 of these stories occurred before Trump finished his first month in office.

The stories are horrible, but the real damage is how the stories are shared across social media. Reputable journalists generate these stories because they *want* them to be true. In their zest to find anything at all that would ridicule or denigrate President Trump, they tweet and share their unsubstantiated opinions, which in turn, is retweeted and shared thousands and thousands of times.

At this point, some of you are questioning the validity of Fake News since these stories are all from

January of 2017. Surely the media is not doing this sort of misreporting anymore.

Let's look at two more recent stories.

Nikki Haley's Extravagant Curtains

In September of 2018, the New York Times ran a story with the headline, "Nikki Haley's View of New York is Priceless. Her Curtains? $52,701". The obvious insinuation being that Nikki Haley, the current US Ambassador to the United Nations, had ordered an extravagant set of curtains for her official New York residence, all on the dime of the American taxpayer.

It was not revealed until the sixth paragraph of the story that the curtains were actually ordered and approved during the final year of the Obama administration.

Once the truth was known and the obvious bias in the headline was called out, The New York Times then changed the headline to read, "State Department Spent $52,701 on Curtains for Nikki Haley's Residence".

An Editor's Note was also added to the story which reads, "An earlier version of this article and headline created an unfair impression about who was responsible for the purchase in question. While Nikki R. Haley is the current ambassador to the United Nations, the decision on leasing the ambassador's residence and purchasing the curtains was made during the Obama administration, according to current and former officials. The article should not have focused on Ms. Haley, nor should a picture of her have been used. The article and headline have now been edited to reflect those concerns, and the picture has been removed."

Once again, the news organization corrects the record, but damage has already been done. The original article never should have run. If The New York Times did their due diligence, and reported facts without their liberal slant, which is what real reporters and news organizations do, then they would have corrected the article *before* it went to print.

Trump's Fist Pump

On September 11, 2018, as the President was walking away from Air Force 1 in Pennsylvania and headed for the crowd that had gathered for a 9/11 service, a picture was taken of the President doing a double fist pump.

The media immediately circulated the photo, which shows Trump throwing his fists up in the air with glee, like a rockstar entering the stage in front of 30,000 screaming fans. The implication of the photo, along with various media taglines, insinuated that Trump was fist pumping the mourning family members of the Flight 93 tragedy.

If you decide to believe the storyline, I suppose you could make it fit. Even though it really makes no sense whatsoever. But that is Trump Derangement Syndrome once again manifesting itself, as people who hate Trump will believe anything, as long as it makes Trump look bad.

Luckily, The Daily Caller did some real reporting, and spoke with a National Guardsman who was at the scene. He said, "The POTUS landed at our Johnstown flight facility, a military installation owned by the Reserves and the National Guard, and, well, prior to his arrival, we were allowed to gather in this designated area to greet him prior to his boarding a helicopter and flying to the Flight 93 memorial service."

This fact is conveniently left out of the double fist pump reporting. The National Guardsman then went on to say, "As he approached us soldiers, marines, and airmen, many were shouting and waving at him. That is when he did the 'double fist pump' — he was genuinely happy to say hello and shake hands, and you could tell he was proud to be greeted by 'his' military members."

This makes sense. So, the Fake News is, "Trump fist pumps mourning family members", but the actual news is, "Trump fist pumps the military in an act of genuine recognition of service and respect for their sacrifice".

As I researched this story, it was very difficult to find the truth, because the liberal news outlets have splattered their biased, speculative, and false comments about the photograph all over the internet.

These stories are all sensational, and the ridiculousness of the content, if they were true, would paint President Trump as a buffoon, racist, or incompetent ass.

If only they were true...

The result of these Fake News stories is hundreds of thousands of people, who rely on these "journalists" for real news, are being fed a pack of lies. These lies then cause people to believe unfavorable and unfair opinions of President Trump based on the Fake News stories.

But that is the point, isn't it? These "reporters" and "journalists" are trying as hard as they can to bring down Donald Trump, even at the expense of their own credibility and principles.

In the end, nothing changes. A fake news story will be shared and retweeted a hundred thousand times, but the tweet or story that explains the lie afterwards will only get shared a dozen times.

Therein lies the problem. These "journalists" are allowed to lie by not following journalistic principles, but are never held accountable. The mainstream media is rife with Trump hating liberals, and the managers and owners of the news organizations where these "journalists" work also want to bring down Trump, so they remain complicit when their underlings report fake stories as fact.

FOX News, on the other hand definitely slants conservative. The big difference being that FOX News still maintains credibility by running stories based on facts.

Almost all of FOX News is arbiters and analysts, offering opinion, insight, guests, and above all, balanced reporting. FOX News rarely has only conservatives in their news blocks. They almost always invite a liberal to offer the arguments of the left, and then given time to state their case. The number of guests is skewed to the right, with more conservatives at any given time, but the liberals are always allowed to make their arguments.

You may have gleaned that I watch FOX News. Yes, I do. I also watch other news stations and am usually disappointed at the unbalanced reporting, as well as the reporting of unverified news stories as fact.

I am not a spokesperson for FOX News, nor am I proposing that everyone should watch. All I am stating is my own opinion, based on my own experiences. If you want the fairest, most balanced, and most accurate news, then FOX News is the news organization that delivers that.

The very loud liberals can make their remarks and be heard by millions of people through media and social media. The only large news organization that actually presents fair and balanced reporting is FOX News, so that means that many people get their news from organizations that already dislike Trump and the conservative point of view.

Unfortunately, I can also tell you from experience, that my liberal friends will not watch FOX News and actually detest it. When I query them on reasoning, it becomes abundantly clear that the one single reason that they have not ever watched, and do not plan on ever watching FOX News, is because they were told that FOX News is the enemy by their usual mainstream news sources, through social media, and most importantly, by their political leaders.

It makes sense that the liberals would not want their constituents to watch FOX News since FOX News does favor the conservative point of view, but reports fairly. The other media channels favor liberals, but to the point that they will omit or misreport information that knowingly and unfairly misrepresents conservatives, conservative issues, and Donald Trump.

President Trump is always portrayed as a buffoon. Mainly because he just doesn't fit the stereotypical leader of the free world. His methods of operation confuse American politicians, confuse world leaders, and confuse the media.

What American politicians and world leaders are quickly finding out, is that he is not a buffoon at all, but more realistically, is quite brilliant. His use of Twitter drives politicians and the media completely insane.

When President Trump gets wind of a Fake News story, he doesn't do like the "good little Republican" of past presidents and sit idly by, taking the "high road" while hoping the fake story goes away, or hoping that the truth will eventually be reported. Past Republican presidents were bashed by the press and never said anything, lest they wouldn't be "presidential".

President Trump broke that mold and stomped it to pieces. He responds to these false stories and sets the record straight. His Tweets aren't the ramblings of a madman, they are the brilliant strategy by the President to communicate to the masses so that the people can know what is really going on.

Instead of letting the liberal media drive the narrative of these fake news stories, Trump uses Twitter as his direct line of communication to the people, completely bypassing the news organizations that generate and propagate these Fake News stories in an attempt to bring down our President and change the political landscape.

In the previous administration, President Obama went to war with Fox News. He didn't like how many of the Fox News stories painted him in an unfavorable light. Fox News did not get in line to tow the liberal narrative for President Obama, so he belittled them and made fun of them.

Without Fox News, would we even know about Benghazi, Uranium One, Fast and Furious, the Hillary

Clinton email investigation, the Clinton Foundation, or the corruption at the Department of Justice?

There are a couple of hosts that are blatantly right wing on Fox News. They sensationalize what they are reporting, but ultimately, the reports are based on facts.

Many liberals, including President Obama, never wanted the facts reported, and definitely do not want their constituents to know the facts. The easiest way to accomplish this for President Obama was to make a joke out of Fox News, which he did masterfully. Many liberals today have never watched anything on Fox News because of President Obama's campaign to ridicule them, which was of course President Obama's goal.

President Trump does the same thing. However, many of the news stories about Trump, as shown above, are completely false. These Fake News stories that are used to disparage President Trump are not based on facts, cannot be corroborated, but are reported anyway.

The old rule of journalism was to find multiple sources. This was required so that one person, who may want to disparage another, could not just make up a story to ruin the other individual.

How easy it would be to just make anything up and then run it as a news story, like "Transgender Teen Suicides Increase When Trump Wins Presidency", or "Bust of Martin Luther King Jr Removed from Oval Office".

Oh wait... those fake stories *were* actually reported as true.

The new rule of liberal journalism is to find the most outrageous story, lead the news with a 5-minute expose', put it on page one, and then let everyone else figure out if it's true.

If it turns out to be false, then offer a 2 second correction or bury a retraction on page 23.

This is precisely how fake news now proliferates. The mainstream media has completely lost all of their journalistic integrity and no longer follow the rules of good journalism.

In the end, how can anyone really blame President Trump for continually calling these news organizations out and setting the record straight?

To Stand or Not to Stand: That Is the Question

According to Forbes, the average pay for an NFL player in the 2015 season was 2.1 million dollars. That means that a player who is not a superstar, but is a decent player, will make about 2.1 million dollars per year.

According to the Unites States Census bureau, the average household income for 2014 was $72, 641. That means that on average, the entire gross pay of a typical family is about 72,461 dollars per year.

Now let's do a little math and put things in perspective. I wonder how long it would take the average American family to make what an average NFL player makes in just one year? If we divide the amount that an NFL player makes in one year, by the amount than an average American family makes in one year, we find that it will take the average American family about 27 years to acquire the income that an NFL player makes in one year. If that NFL player plays two years, and we stipulate that the average American works from eighteen years old to sixty-seven years old, then that NFL player will make more in two years than the average American family in their entire lifetime.

Of course, the pay will increase for our American family, but so will the NFL players salary.

This large disparity in pay is part of the reason that many fans of the NFL take issue with the player's stance on kneeling or pointing fists in NFL games. These players are great athletes, no doubt about it. But that's all they are.

Their pay is part of supply and demand. The NFL created a huge money-making enterprise. Ticket costs and merchandise are very expensive. The reason that the players, who are only the pawns of the owners, can command such high wages only highlights the amount of money that is being made by the NFL as a whole. The reason that the NFL exists at all, is because we the fans have decided that the cost for tickets and merchandise is worth it.

What the NFL refuses to realize, is that we the fans can just as easily spend our money elsewhere.

Since the NFL is a private company, then I firmly believe that they can do as they wish when it comes to players standing during the National Anthem. If they want to allow the players to stand, then they can stand. If the NFL wants the players to be respectful of the flag and the National Anthem, then they can impose punishments up to and including termination if the players refuse to stand, That is wholly up to the NFL.

On the other hand, we are consumers of the NFL, and just like the supplier and consumer of any arrangement, we, as the consumer, can choose not to purchase the product or service if it does not comply with our own standards.

If my local restaurant has been serving me satisfactorily for years, I will go back. If I go again, and the waiter or waitress is rude, or if the food is below par, or the tables are not clean, then I have three choices. I can keep quiet and hope that things return to normal, I can just leave and never come back, or I can offer a constructive complaint so that the owner is aware that there is a problem.

The way that I would handle it, is to give it one more chance. If I return and nothing has changed, then I will offer my constructive criticism to the manager. If the manager is rude, or if I return and nothing has changed, then I will not go back.

I have had to make these types of restaurant choices many times during my life, I have had instances where the restaurant self-corrected, and I continued going back without ever having to say a word. I have had instances where the manager became defensive and combative, or paid lip service but never fixed the problem, and I never went back. I have also had instances where the manager listened thoughtfully, took corrective action, and I still frequent these restaurants to this day.

Restaurants can do whatever they like. They can choose to treat me poorly, and I can in turn, choose to not spend my money and eat dinner there.

The main point here, is that the NFL can take corrective action, do nothing, or become combative regarding customer complaints related to the players standing during the National Anthem.

In their defense, they did attempt to take corrective action and impose penalties for those that elected to stay on the field and protest, but the player's union took action to block it. The player's union, which exists to bargain for and help the player's receive equitable contracts, dropped the ball on this one. Or should I say, fumbled the ball.

Viewership has decreased over the past few years. Maybe it was going to happen anyway, but I firmly believe that protesting during the National Anthem played a large role in the decline in viewership. I myself was an avid fan until this all started two years ago, and I have lost interest. Last year I watched only three complete games.

Some people may ask, but why would the National Anthem protests affect me so much that I don't want to watch the game? After all, it's only a couple of minutes at the start of the game.

After giving this some careful consideration, I think the prime reasons are the supposed motive for the protests, which is police brutality, and for the elitist attitude of the players.

These players claim to care about the less privileged people of their community. Yet, instead of actually doing something about it, like engaging with the president and actually trying to generate some needed reform, they would rather stick their finger in the eye of the people who pay their salaries.

I believe that these athletes could do an immense amount of good in the inner cities and to be role models for the young impressionable children who live there. Many athletes do, but most don't.

When I watch a game, I don't want to witness any of these wealthy, spoiled, privileged players protest anything. Least of all, something that they are getting wrong. As I picture them driving home in their hundred thousand-dollar cars and sleeping in their multimillion-dollar homes, the last thing I want to see is them protesting the very people who gave them these incredible opportunities.

The players should be celebrating the police and our military, and paying respect to their sacrifice every game. The NFL players might have to go home with a pulled hamstring, while the military and police may never get to go home at all.

As I described in the chapter, "ICE, the Police, and Other Heroes", the statistics show that shootings by police based on race is nearly identical to the number of violent crimes perpetrated by race.

So there really is no argument for these athletes. I understand that some police may be racist, and that some police may be brutal in their tactics. These police should be rooted out and punished, with jail time if required.

However, the vast majority of police are decent, selfless individuals who serve with honor and integrity. If the players would start a campaign to honor the police, and teach our younger generation about the sacrifice of our police every single day, rather than painting them all with one broad brush as power mad racists, then perhaps we can begin moving the police, our perception of the police, and our community in a more peaceful direction.

Why Polls Don't Matter

The divide between Democrat and Republican, thanks to the divisive political style of President Obama, has never been more evident.

There have always been differences. That's why the two parties exist. But the differences were always tempered by the things we had in common.

Simple things like love of country, respect for the police, respect for the military, allegiance to the flag, respect for elders, and pride in America would always reground the political differences.

This is no longer the case. Among liberals, respect for anything is all but gone. The emphasis is always on the individual. Lately, the liberal mantra has been that hundreds, thousands, and millions must suffer, so that one individual can feel "comfortable".

For some inane reason, they have moved to a position that if one person "feels" uncomfortable, then that uncomfortable feeling must be removed, even if it is at the expense of thousands feeling uncomfortable as a result.

This type of thinking drives the liberal position of entitlement. Where no one should ever have to feel uncomfortable. Where everything should be free. Healthcare should be free; Education should be free; Food should be free; Housing should be free.

Evidently, when the left added this entitlement culture to the curriculum at our schools, they must have removed mathematics and economics to make room, because the math just doesn't work.

The more people that receive entitlements, means that less people are working. As the workers observe the new culture warriors sitting at home playing video games and surviving for "free' without working, then the workers will begin to wonder why *they* are working.

Eventually, the workers will stop this stupidity of working and join the ranks of the entitlement receiving culture warriors. Ultimately, everyone is happily sitting at home, doing no work, and receiving everything for free.

Utopia has finally arrived.

Except, nothing is for free. If someone is getting something for free, then someone else is paying for it. There are no free rides, and Socialism can never work.

But these young adults today don't know that. Frankly, they don't seem to know much of anything except that they must resist the people who are actually working for a living.

Meanwhile, the workers have realized that the Liberals are in fact trying to take their money and redistribute it to the non-workers, thus the 2016 general election upset.

The workers were not happy, and in an attempt to restore order and move the country back to greatness, elected Donald Trump.

These people who have elected Donald Trump found out long before the general election in 2016, that by displaying their political affiliation with Donald Trump, they were being ridiculed, attacked, spat on, and worse by the entitled young adults.

Here are some examples:

In May of 2018, two workers at a Cheesecake Factory Restaurant made disparaging remarks to a patron wearing a MAGA hat (Make America Great Again hat). The patron reportedly stated that the workers were making threatening remarks and balling their fists to scare him. The Cheesecake Factory immediately fired the two workers.

In July of 2018, a video went viral showing a 30-year-old man verbally assaulting three teenagers at a San Antonio Whataburger. The man approached the youths, including one wearing a MAGA hat, and threw a drink in the boy's faces. Then ripped the MAGA hat off of the boy's head, ripping some hair out along with it. The man was arrested and said that the MAGA hat had the same effect on him as a Ku Klux Klan hood.

In July of 2018, a Capitol Hill intern and his colleagues were denied service by an Uber driver because they were wearing MAGA hats. Uber is looking into it.

In August, 2018, a student at Union Mine High School in El Dorado, California, snatched a MAGA hat off of the head of another student while shouting profanities while in class. The teacher banished the teacher from the class but the student returned a second time and snatched the hat off a second time. The teacher was slapped by the student while attempting to keep the student away.

You get the idea. People who wear MAGA hats do so at their own peril.

That's because the left has become completely unhinged. The young liberals and their support for groups like Antifa, are now threatening people with violence if they display support for Donald Trump.

In the adult world of over thirty, the same thing is happening. People are afraid to show their support of Donald Trump lest they be ostracized or worse.

Restaurant owners are publicly shaming patrons who work for Trump. In June of 2018, Sarah Huckabee Sanders, the White House Press Secretary, was driven out of the Red Hen Restaurant in Lexington, Virginia, by the owner because she worked for Donald Trump.

This is the "tolerance" of the liberal left. They hate Donald Trump so much, that they channel that hate to anyone who supports him. If you publicly show your support for Donald Trump, you risk being shamed, verbally attacked, and asked to leave, or worse.

Most Trump supporters are older and have the benefit of life experience. They know what the ramifications will be if they publicly profess that they support Trump and they are not foolish enough to risk the consequences. These supporters are also smart enough to realize that social media, phone records, and other forms of electronic communications make them susceptible to liberal outrage if the admit that they support President Trump.

More recently, Twitter CEO, Jack Dorsey, said in an interview that people in his company that have conservative views do not feel safe to express their opinions. Specifically, Dorsey told Jay Rosen in an interview published by Recode, "We have a lot of conservative-leaning folks in the company as well, and to be honest, they don't feel safe to express their opinions at the company".

This tells you everything you need to know about why polls no longer matter. Liberals are so maniacal and violent in their hatred for Trump and his supporters, that regular, everyday folks who happen to politically agree with the president are so fearful from liberal retribution, that they cannot make their actual opinions known.

I have said this several times and it is worth repeating. In their zeal to bypass the will of the people, the socialists and liberals who completely detest Trump and his supporters, attempt to silence conservative opinions through intimidation, fear, public shaming and violence.

This is exactly what is happening at Twitter and it is happening in companies across America. It is interesting that the news continually reports that these companies like Twitter are left-leaning and that most of the workers are liberal.

But why would that be a given? If conservatives are fearful of losing their jobs or fearful of being attacked, either physically or through public shaming, then how do we really know how many conservatives are in the company?

Another interesting thought is: If these conservatives are "pretending" to be liberal so that they don't lose their jobs, then how does that affect their work? The logical conclusion is that these people are probably making decisions that they don't agree with and actually go against their principles.

I know that many of you would say that these people should stand up for their principles and quit. Make a statement by leaving the company.

There are at least two things wrong with this point of view.

First, these people were hired because they have the ability to do a job. Liberals are, and rightly so, always claiming that our work environments should be discrimination free. So why then, would we allow people to be hired, fired, or driven out of their job just because they have a different political point of view? This is classic discrimination and is not different than claiming you can't work here because men are not secretaries, or you can't work here because women are not engineers.

Second, these people have worked hard to earn their positions. Why, just because of discrimination and fear, should they be forced to leave a decent paying job and put the security of their family at risk?

It is easy to understand why the conservatives pretend to be liberals. It is also an easy transition from the workplace to the polling place.

So, what happens when a pollster calls a Trump supporter and asks who they are voting for? The Trump supporter knows that if they give an honest answer, then they risk retribution from the left.

The Trump supporter is also intelligent enough to realize that this poll means nothing, and their answering honestly has no real gain. It's a meaningless number for the media to tout one candidate over another. In the end, the Trump supporter chooses safety. He chooses no risk. He chooses the liberal candidate for the pollster.

The same is true on exit polls. Many Trump supporters will not risk the violent reactions of the left if they are discovered to support President Trump. So they tell a little white lie and say they voted for the Democrat when exiting the polling station.

No harm, no foul. Their vote counts for the real conservative candidate, and they can walk away without fear of being publicly shamed, spat on, or worse.

At least for the moment, at this particular time in history, the polls will never reflect reality.

The Benghazi Attacks

On September 11, 2012, the US Mission in Benghazi was attacked at 9:42pm. Seven and a half hours later, at about 5:15am, a second US facility was attacked. Two Americans, US Ambassador Christopher Stevens and State Department computer expert Sean Smith are killed in the initial assault, and two more Americans, former Navy Seals and contractors, Tyrone Woods and Glen Doherty are killed in the second assault.

Most of us have heard the story. It was blamed by the Obama State Department as local retaliation to a video that supposedly caused the locals to revolt.

It was finally determined, however, to be a terrorist attack. When Hillary Clinton was asked by the House Committee on Benghazi if the attack was because of a video or because of a terrorist attack, her response was:

"With all due respect, the fact is we had four dead Americans. Was it because of a protest, or was it because of guys out for a walk one night who decided they'd go kill some Americans? What difference, at this point, does it make? It our job to figure out what happened and do everything we can to prevent it from ever happening again, senator. Now, honestly, I will do my best to answer your questions about this. The fact is that people were trying, in real time, to get to the best information."

Yes, what difference, at this point, does it make? Dead is dead, right? Four dead Americans. Tdailyhe So, let's just forget about the details and just move on.

I'm sorry Secretary Clinton, but it does make a difference. Finding out why four Americans died is very important. Especially if they died for nothing and if their deaths could have been prevented.

Two months before the attacks, Christopher Stevens requested extra security personnel. He said a minimum of thirteen would be required. The Hillary Clinton State Department turned him down.

I wonder how many paid personnel, security and non-security, surrounded Clinton at the time? I bet she was fully staffed.

But even more important, is one thing that has always bothered me about the events of that night. And that is the timeline.

The first attack occurred at 9:42pm. The second attack was at 5:15am, over seven hours later.

Think about that for a moment. Any of us who have travelled understand what seven hours means. I can fly on a commercial airline from Boston, Massachusetts, to San Francisco, California in six hours and twenty-two minutes. I can fly from Boston, Massachusetts, to Munich, Germany, a trip of 3,851 miles across the Atlantic Ocean, in seven hours and fifteen minutes.

Leon Panetta, the Secretary of Defense at the time, said that there were no US military aircraft in the area to be deployed at the time of the attack. The closest was in Rota, Spain, he claimed.

The point-to-point distance from Rota, Spain to Benghazi, Libya is 1,535 miles. Commercial flight time would be 3.5 hours.

The Daily Mail reported that between midnight and 2am, Panetta told two Marine anti-terrorism teams based in Rota, Spain to prepare to deploy to Libya.

Really? He knew the consulate was under attack, and it took more than two hours to *prepare* to deploy a rescue team?

Are we really supposed to believe that the State Department was not able to provide any kind of military response in 7.5 hours? The greatest, strongest, most technically advanced country in the world could not provide air cover to its citizens in less than 7.5 hours?

Why were no jets scrambled? Why did it take so long to send the rescue team?

I have heard the excuses. The fighter jets don't have the range. The base in Italy wouldn't have been able to scramble the jets quickly.

But these are only excuses made by politicians. If the decisions were in the hands of the military, fighter jets would have been doing flyovers of Benghazi in a few hours and the second attack would most likely have been prevented. But the decision was not in the hands of the military, it was in the hands of the politicians at the State Department.

The liberal excuse that I find most disturbing, is that there wasn't enough time for assets to arrive anyway, so the decision not to attempt a flyover with fighter jets would have been pointless.

Let's give them the benefit of the doubt and say, for arguments sake, that they tried to scramble the jets and they really didn't make it in time.

Then the politicians would have an argument. At least they could have said that they tried. But their real argument is based on hindsight. They are saying that, based on the timeline that we now know, there wouldn't have been enough time anyway.

But what if the second attack happened 8 hours later, or 9 hours later?

The fact that the politicians so eloquently avoid, is that they didn't even try.

The bottom line on Benghazi, is that Obama's State Department and Defense Department were either completely incompetent, or they wanted to hide the fact that there was another terrorist attack because it was so close to the 2012 general elections.

I am not a conspiracy theorist, but I don't believe that all of the people involved were incompetent. What then remains is politics.

When you seriously look at the timeline, it is clear that decisions were not made, or decisions were delayed, because of politics. The deaths of at least two Americans occurred because of politics.

The United States has the most advanced military in the world. When I hear President Obama or Hillary Clinton speak about Benghazi, I don't want to hear the excuses of why they believe nothing could be done, I want to know why they didn't even try.

The Electoral College

We hear it from the Democrats incessantly since the 2016 general election with their loss to Donald Trump, when Hillary Clinton won the popular vote. We heard it before in the 2000 presidential election when George W. Bush defeated Al Gore, winning the electoral vote but losing the popular vote.

How can this be, decry the left? How can someone win the popular vote and still lose the election. This is simply not democratic, is the rallying cry.

The young liberals throw their hands to the sky and yell, "Don't we live in a democracy?"

Ummm... No, young liberals, no we don't. We live in a republic.

From the Oxford Dictionary: a republic is a country in which supreme power is held by the people and their elected representatives, and which has an elected or nominated president rather than a monarch.

In the republic system of the United States, rather than have the entire population determine the outcome of elections, we locally elect representatives to make decisions about the government. To further complicate things, the republic system of the United States also has individual states that are autonomous from each other.

These distinguishing features were not lost on the Founding Fathers. In fact, they designed it this way to ensure equality.

Equality in the US Republic was designed so that all people get a voice within their individual states, and then that all states get a voice in the overall republic.

If we did not have the electoral system for presidential elections, then the population centers would quickly take control and never relinquish it.

Since many of the Democrat states are high population states, like California, New York, and Illinois, the Democrats would love to change to the popular vote system of voting. The high population, liberal slanted states would remove the voice of the less populated states.

The Founding Fathers utilized the same thinking for Congress. That's why all states have an equal number of only two senators. The House of Representatives is uneven and weighted according to population. But the Senate equalizes the numbers so that all states can have fair representation.

To show how brilliant the Founding Fathers were to ensure equality in the presidential elections, all we have to do is look at the most populous state, California, and the least populous state, Wyoming.

California is roughly twice the land area of Wyoming, but has about 69 times the population. As of

2018, California has a population of about 39,776,830, Wyoming has a population of about 573,720, and the total United States population is about 328,032,421.

If we use the voting process of popular vote, then each state would contribute their votes directly compared to the total population.

So, California contributes 12.13% of all possible votes in the United States. Wyoming contributes 0.17% of all possible votes in the United States. In fact, California's vote completely swamps out the 21 least populous states plus Washington DC. The total population of these states and Washington DC is only 37.364,699, with their total vote contribution at 11.39%.

30	Iowa	3160553
31	Utah	3159345
32	Nevada	3056824
33	Arkansas	3020327
34	Mississippi	2982785
35	Kansas	2918515
36	New Mexico	2090708
37	Nebraska	1932549
38	West Virginia	1803077
39	Idaho	1753860
40	Hawaii	1426393
41	New Hampshire	1350575
42	Maine	1341582
43	Montana	1062330
44	Rhode Island	1061712
45	Delaware	971180
46	South Dakota	877790
47	North Dakota	755238
48	Alaska	738068
49	District of Columbia	703608
50	Vermont	623960
51	Wyoming	573720

So, in a true democracy, rather than a republic, the high population states completely negate the least populous states and the least populous states completely lose their voice in the democratic process.

The Founding Fathers understood this and knew that the population centers would control the presidency if the presidency was decided by the popular vote. So, in their infinite wisdom, the Founding Fathers created the Electoral College as a means of electing the president. This ensured equality among the states and it ensures that every state has a voice.

The Electoral College still favors high population states, because the higher the population, the more Electoral Votes that state receives.

But, to bring equity to the less populated states, the number of Electoral Votes of each state is equal to the sum of their Representatives and Senators. Since every state has at least one Representative and two Senators, then every state is guaranteed at least three Electoral Votes. Thus, California has 55 Electoral Votes and Wyoming has 3.

At first, this doesn't seem like much of a difference. But now, if we look at the percentage contribution of each state with respect to the total Electoral College Votes of 538, then we see that the Founding Fathers were indeed brilliant.

Now California contributes 10.22% of all possible electoral votes in the United States, which is 2% less than a true democracy, while Wyoming now contributes 0.56% of all possible electoral votes in the United States, which is 3.3 times more than a true democracy. When we consider the same 21 least populous states plus Washington DC, these states now contribute 17.66% of the Electoral College votes, which is 6.27% more than a true democracy.

In a true democracy, California silences the voice of 21 other states. In a republic with the Electoral College, those 21 states still have a voice.

Before everyone screams about the numbers, I am completely aware that I am including all citizens in my analysis, even those that are too young to vote. However, I am making an assumption that the child to adult ratio does not change much from state to state, so the numbers will still be close.

Regardless, this exercise is really about why the Electoral College is required and less about the actual final numbers.

In our system of government, where the individual states maintain their autonomy, we must ensure that they have a voice in presidential elections so that their local needs are met. California dictating what happens in Wyoming cannot be acceptable since the needs of Wyoming are entirely different than the needs of California.

The Founding Fathers were brilliant indeed.

What Has Trump Done Anyway?

The Washington Examiner has reported The White House's list of 52 accomplishments of the Trump Administration during its nearly first 600 days:

- Almost 4 million jobs created since election.
- More Americans are now employed than ever recorded before in our history.
- We have created more than 400,000 manufacturing jobs since my election.
- Manufacturing jobs growing at the fastest rate in more than THREE DECADES.
- Economic growth last quarter hit 4.2 percent.
- New unemployment claims recently hit a 49-year low.
- Median household income has hit highest level ever recorded.
- African-American unemployment has recently achieved the lowest rate ever recorded.
- Hispanic-American unemployment is at the lowest rate ever recorded.
- Asian-American unemployment recently achieved the lowest rate ever recorded.

- Women's unemployment recently reached the lowest rate in 65 years.
- Youth unemployment has recently hit the lowest rate in nearly half a century.
- Lowest unemployment rate ever recorded for Americans without a high school diploma
- Under my Administration, veterans' unemployment recently reached its lowest rate in nearly 20 years.
- Almost 3.9 million Americans have been lifted off food stamps since the election.
- The Pledge to America's Workers has resulted in employers committing to train more than 4 million Americans. We are committed to VOCATIONAL education.
- 95 percent of U.S. manufacturers are optimistic about the future—highest ever.
- Retail sales surged last month, up another 6% over last year.
- Signed the biggest package of tax cuts and reforms in history. After tax cuts, over $300 billion dollars poured back in to the U.S. in the first quarter alone.
- As a result of our tax bill, small businesses will have the lowest top marginal tax rate in more than 80 years.

- Helped win U.S. bid for the 2028 Summer Olympics in Los Angeles.
- Helped win U.S.-Mexico-Canada's united bid for 2026 World Cup.
- Opened ANWR & Approved Keystone XL and Dakota Access Pipelines.
- Record number of regulations eliminated.
- Enacted regulatory relief for community banks and credit unions.
- Obamacare individual mandate penalty GONE.
- My Administration is providing more affordable healthcare options for Americans through association health plans and short-term duration plans.
- Last month, the FDA approved more affordable generic drugs than ever before in history. And thanks to our efforts, many drug companies are freezing or reversing planned price increases.
- We reformed the Medicare program to stop hospitals from overcharging low-income seniors on their drugs--saving seniors hundreds of millions of dollars this year alone.
- Signed Right-To-Try Legislation.

- Secured $6 billion dollars in NEW funding to fight the opioid epidemic.
- We have reduced high-dose opioid prescriptions by 16% during my first year in office.
- Signed VA Choice Act and VA Accountability Act, expanded VA telehealth services, walk-in-clinics and same-day urgent primary and mental health care.
- Increased our coal exports by 60%; U.S. oil production recently reached all-time high.
- United States is a net natural gas exporter for the first time since 1957.
- Withdrew the United States from the job-killing Paris Climate Accord.
- Cancelled the illegal, anti-coal, so-called Clean Power Plan.
- Secured record $700 billion dollars in military funding; $716 billion next year.
- NATO allies are spending $69 billion dollars more on defense since 2016.
- Process has begun to make the Space Force the 6th branch of the armed forces.
- Confirmed more circuit court judges than any other new administration.
- Confirmed Supreme Court Justice Neil Gorsuch; Nominated Judge Brett Kavanagh.

- Withdrew from the horrible, one-sided Iran Deal.
- Moved U.S. Embassy to Jerusalem.
- Protecting Americans from terrorists with the Travel Ban, upheld by Supreme Court.
- Issued executive order to keep open Guantanamo Bay.
- Concluded an historic U.S.-Mexico Trade Deal to replace NAFTA. And negotiations with Canada are underway as we speak.
- Reached a breakthrough agreement with the EU to increase U.S. exports.
- Imposed tariffs on foreign Steel & Aluminum to protect our national security.
- Imposed tariffs on China in response to China's forced technology transfer, intellectual property theft, and their chronically abusive trade practices.
- Net exports are on track to increase by $59 billion dollars this year.
- Improved vetting & screening for refugees, and switched focus to overseas resettlement.
- We have begun BUILDING THE WALL. Republicans want STRONG BORDERS and NO CRIME. Democrats want OPEN BORDERS which equals MASSIVE CRIME.

References

Blaze, The
https://www.theblaze.com/news/2018/08/05/sen-dianne-feinstein-responds-to-report-about-staffer-being-a-chinese-spy-by-attacking-trump

Business Insider
https://www.businessinsider.com/chinese-white-collar-criminals-death-sentence-2013-7#luo-yaping-executed-2

https://www.businessinsider.com/who-else-was-in-the-room-when-trump-jr-met-with-the-russian-lawyer-2017-7

https://www.businessinsider.com/lawyers-robert-mueller-hired-for-the-trump-russia-investigation-2017-6#andrew-weissmann-2

https://www.businessinsider.com/cheryl-mills-and-clinton-staffers-granted-immunity-by-the-fbi-2016-9

https://www.businessinsider.com/cheesecake-factory-suspends-workers-after-maga-hat-incident-2018-5

CBS News

https://www.cbsnews.com/pictures/the-most-dangerous-cities-in-america/

CNN
http://www.cnn.com/2009/US/07/22/harvard.gates.interview/

https://www.cnn.com/2017/09/19/politics/read-michael-cohen-statement/index.html

https://www.cnn.com/2013/09/10/world/benghazi-consulate-attack-fast-facts/index.html

Daily Caller, The
http://dailycaller.com/2018/06/14/msnbc-migrant-children-detention-cages/

http://dailycaller.com/2018/02/21/exclusive-zero-registered-republicans-mueller-lawyer/

http://dailycaller.com/2018/05/03/mueller-lawyer-hillary-clinton/

https://dailycaller.com/2018/09/13/natl-guardsman-debunks-biased-media/

Daily Mail, The

http://www.dailymail.co.uk/news/article-2230779/Leon-Panetta-says-NOT-military-planes-near-Libya-stopped-Benghazi-attack.html

Department of Justice, The
https://www.bjs.gov/content/pub/pdf/rhovo1215.pdf

Epoch Times, The
https://www.theepochtimes.com/strzok-joins-list-of-25-top-fbi-doj-officials-who-have-been-recently-fired-demoted-or-resigned_2624607.html

Factcheck.org
https://www.factcheck.org/2018/05/qa-on-stormy-daniels-payment/

FBI.gov
https://www.fbi.gov/news/pressrel/press-releases/statement-by-fbi-director-james-b-comey-on-the-investigation-of-secretary-hillary-clinton2019s-use-of-a-personal-e-mail-system

Federalist, The
http://thefederalist.com/2017/02/06/16-fake-news-stories-reporters-have-run-since-trump-won/

Forbes

https://www.forbes.com/lists/2005/54/Rank_1.html

https://www.forbes.com/sites/chasewithorn/2015/09/29/2015-forbes-400-full-list-of-americas-richest-people/#735dfe8b3c64

https://www.forbes.com/sites/kurtbadenhausen/2016/12/15/average-player-salaries-in-major-american-sports-leagues/#371ab9d01050

Fox News
http://www.foxnews.com/entertainment/2018/09/14/new-york-times-admits-creating-unfair-impression-about-nikki-haleys-53g-curtains-that-were-okd-by-obama-administration.html

Guardian, The
https://www.theguardian.com/world/2018/aug/12/white-supremacist-rally-unite-the-right-washington-dc

https://www.theguardian.com/us-news/2016/aug/20/us-navy-sailor-jailed-for-taking-photos-of-classified-areas-of-nuclear-submarine

Heritage Foundation, The
https://www.heritage.org/immigration/commentary/daca-unconstitutional-obama-admitted

Hill, The
http://thehill.com/homenews/senate/406697-rubio-defends-haley-over-curtains-story-example-of-media-pushing-bias

ICE
https://www.ice.gov/

Justice.gov
https://www.justice.gov/file/1007346/download

Last Refuge, The
https://theconservativetreehouse.com/2018/05/04/breaking-former-fbi-chief-legal-counsel-james-baker-resigns-from-fbi-granular-detail-indicates-no-immunity/

LifeZette
https://www.lifezette.com/2018/07/maga-hat-thief-is-arrested-after-lousy-incident-texas/

Mark Humphrys
http://markhumphrys.com/media.obama.html

MSNBC
http://www.msnbc.com/rachel-maddow-show/what-difference-point-does-it

New American, The
https://www.thenewamerican.com/usnews/politics/item/28530-why-mccabe-was-fired

New York Post, The
https://nypost.com/2016/09/23/cheryl-mills-given-immunity-deal-in-clinton-email-server-probe/

New York Times, The
https://www.nytimes.com/2017/12/01/us/politics/michael-flynn-guilty-russia-investigation.html

https://www.nytimes.com/2016/09/09/us/politics/hillary-clinton-emails-investigation.html

https://www.nytimes.com/2016/11/11/us/politics/the-electoral-college-is-hated-by-many-so-why-does-it-endure.html?action=click&module=RelatedCoverage&pgtype=Article&region=Footer

New Yorker, The
https://www.newyorker.com/news/news-desk/donald-trump-a-playboy-model-and-a-system-for-concealing-infidelity-national-enquirer-karen-mcdougal

Pew Reasearch

http://www.pewresearch.org/fact-tank/2017/02/15/u-s-students-internationally-math-science/

PJ Media
https://pjmedia.com/trending/the-real-reason-why-the-fbi-had-a-spy-in-the-trump-campaign/

Politico
https://www.politico.com/story/2013/01/obama-2008-campaign-fined-375000-085784

https://www.politico.com/story/2018/03/09/donald-trump-kristian-saucier-pardon-450484

Recode
https://www.recode.net/2018/9/14/17857486/twitter-jack-dorsey-nyu-jay-rosen-bias-neutrality-presence-politics-recode-media-podcast

Roll Call
https://www.rollcall.com/news/politics/every-member-congress-wealth-one-chart

Sharyl Attkisson
https://sharylattkisson.com/2017/12/25/investigating-the-investigators-at-doj-and-fbi/

Splinter News
https://splinternews.com/capitol-hill-interns-with-maga-hats-say-uber-driver-ref-1827616783

Townhall
https://townhall.com/columnists/charleskrauthammer/2003/12/05/bush-derangement-syndrome-n940041

USA Today
https://www.usatoday.com/story/news/politics/2018/06/23/trump-spokeswoman-sarah-sanders-virginia-restaurant/727972002/

Washington Examiner
https://www.washingtonexaminer.com/washington-secrets/list-white-house-touts-53-accomplishments-woodward-ignored

Washington Post, The
https://www.washingtonpost.com/investigations/nationwide-police-shot-and-killed-nearly-1000-people-in-2017/2018/01/04/4eed5f34-e4e9-11e7-ab50-621fe0588340_story.html?utm_term=.f0d0d0e91a29

Wikipedia
https://en.m.wikipedia.org/wiki/Household_income_in_the_United_States

https://en.wikipedia.org/wiki/Electoral_College_(United_States)